Cognitive Grammar in Stylistics

Cognitive Grammar in Stylistics

A Practical Guide

Marcello Giovanelli and Chloe Harrison

BLOOMSBURY ACADEMIC

LONDON • NEW YORK • OXFORD • NEW DELHI • SYDNEY

BLOOMSBURY ACADEMIC
Bloomsbury Publishing Plc
50 Bedford Square, London, WC1B 3DP, UK
1385 Broadway, New York, NY 10018, USA

BLOOMSBURY, BLOOMSBURY ACADEMIC and the Diana logo are trademarks
of Bloomsbury Publishing Plc

First published in Great Britain 2018

Cover design: Olivia D'Cruz
Cover image © Getty Images/Gary Waters

A catalogue record for this book is available from the British Library.

Library of Congress Cataloging-in-Publication Data
Names: Giovanelli, Marcello, author. | Harrison, Chloe, author.
Title: Cognitive grammar in stylistics: a practical guide / by Marcello Giovanelli
and Chloe Harrison.
Description: London: Bloomsbury Publishing, [2018] | Includes
bibliographical references and index.
Identifiers: LCCN 2018002421 (print) | LCCN 2018005982 (ebook) |
ISBN 9781474298933 (ePDF) | ISBN 9781474298940 (ePub) | ISBN 9781474298919
(softcover) | ISBN 9781474298926 (hardcover) | ISBN 9781474298940 (ebook)
Subjects: LCSH: Cognitive grammar. | Grammar, Comparative and general–Style. |
Language and languages–Style. | Creativity (Linguistics)
Classification: LCC P165 (ebook) | LCC P165 .C639 2018 (print) | DDC
415.01/835–dc23
LC record available at https://lccn.loc.gov/2018002421

ISBN: HB: 978-1-4742-9892-6
PB: 978-1-4742-9891-9
ePDF: 978-1-4742-9893-3
eBook: 978-1-4742-9894-0

Typeset by Deanta Global Publishing Services, Chennai, India
Printed and bound in Great Britain

To find out more about our authors and books visit www.bloomsbury.com
and sign up for our newsletters.

Contents

List of figures and tables

Acknowledgements

We would like to thank Furzeen Ahmed, Sam Browse, Urszula Clark, Ian Cushing and Louise Nuttall who read an early manuscript of this book and provided us with helpful feedback and insightful suggestions for improvement. We are also grateful to Gurdeep Mattu and Helen Saunders at Bloomsbury for all of their support at various stages of writing.

We would also like to thank the following for permission to reproduce copyright material: Text 2I: Advertisement for a professional training course reprinted by permission of SPE International: Aberdeen Section ©2013. Text 4E: Pages 1–3 from *Funnybones: The Pet Shop* by Allan Ahlberg and Andre Amstutz (Puffin, 2004) Copyright ©Allan Ahlberg, 1980. Reproduced by permission of Penguin Books Ltd.; Text 4F: Cartoon reprinted by permission of Rob Tornoe ©2015; Text 4H: 'Words' [20 1. Complete, 4 1. repeated in analysis] from *Ariel: Poems* by Sylvia Plath. Copyright © 1961, 1962, 1963, 1964, 1965, 1966 by Ted Hughes. Reprinted by permission of HarperCollins Publishers and Faber and Faber Ltd.; Text 8I: 'Catching Fire'; re-printed with permission of Nigel McLoughlin; Image 8L: From *The Rime of the Modern Mariner* by Nick Hayes, published by Jonathan Cape. Reproduced by permission of The Random House Group Ltd. ©2011.

While every effort has been made to contact copyright holders, we would be pleased to hear of any that have been omitted and would be happy to include the appropriate acknowledgements on reprinting.

Chapter 1
Introduction

Key objectives

In this chapter we will explore:

- the general aims and principles of stylistics as a discipline;
- the different models of grammars that have been used in stylistics; and
- some overarching principles of cognitive grammar.

1.1 Aims of this book

In this book, we aim to provide an engaging, accessible and practically focused introduction to cognitive grammar in stylistics by demonstrating cognitive grammar's key principles and concepts, and explaining how these can be used to support stylistic analyses of a range of literary and non-literary texts. In each chapter, we hope to demonstrate that cognitive grammar offers a powerful alternative to more traditional grammatical models in supporting you to critically examine a variety of different text types.

This book is aimed mainly at undergraduates taking courses in English language, linguistics, stylistics or literary studies. Given that courses vary from institution to institution and that students arrive onto programmes with different backgrounds, experience and knowledge, we have assumed no prior knowledge of either linguistics or stylistics. Furthermore, since cognitive grammar is a relatively new method of analysis in stylistics, we provide a step-by-step account both of some of its central premises and concepts and of its potential to help you explore, interpret and evaluate texts. Throughout the book, we therefore take a practical approach, exemplifying cognitive grammar *in action* and offering activities designed to get you working with and exploring its principles in your own analyses.

1.2 Stylistics

1.2.1 Doing stylistics

As the title of this book suggests, our focus is on outlining cognitive grammar as a method of stylistic practice. Doing stylistics and being a stylistician start from the premise that whenever we read a text, our initial engagement with that text is on a *linguistic* level. That is, we are responding to the language choices and patterns as an integral part of how we make meaning. An idea central to stylistics, then, is that any analysis we undertake should be grounded in as precise a description and discussion of language as is possible, drawing on the most relevant and up-to-date models and ideas from linguistics to help us to do so. Typically, these can be from a number of different theoretical and methodological positions and may involve examining language at a number of different language levels: lexis, grammar, semantics, phonology, discourse and pragmatics.

There are some important caveats here. First, being a stylistician does not mean simply resorting to labelling and counting up features in a text. Stylistics is not about describing the linguistic properties of a poem or an advertisement or an extract from a novel with little attention to how those features give rise to a particular interpretation. Instead, stylisticians engage with and explicitly identify the readings that emerge from a reader or groups of readers engaging with those linguistic features. They also consider the various contexts in which texts are produced and received as a way of illuminating analysis and discussion. This means that it is perfectly possible, and indeed wholly desirable, for stylistic analyses to draw on biographical, historical, cultural and generic factors in conjunction with a close language-focused approach.

A second important caveat is centred in the notion of meaning itself. It is important to remember that the linguistic features of any text depend on the wider co-text (the surrounding thematic and structural elements) and the context (how, where and by whom the text is produced and read), which together provide a frame that can afford and/or constrain interpretations. This means that it is theoretically and methodologically impossible to make the claim that a single linguistic feature gives rise to a particular effect in *all* situations. For example, look at Text 1A, the famous lines from Book One of William Wordsworth's *The Prelude*, where the speaker is describing skating at night.

Text 1A

All shod with steel,
We hissed along the polished ice in games

(Wordsworth [1850] 1995)

In these lines, the repetition of the sounds /sh/ and /s/ in 'shod', 'steel', 'hissed', 'polished', 'ice' and 'games' foregrounds and, in this instance, appears to mirror the sound of skates gliding across ice. Reading these lines, it is possible to argue that they evoke a demonstrable effect but it would be wrong to assert that this gliding sound was an attribute independent of the context in which /sh/ and /s/ appear. You can easily prove this by collecting countless examples of where it would be difficult or plain wrong to suggest that these sounds produce the effect of gliding.

1.2.2 Avoiding impressionism

A primary aim for the stylistician, then, is to avoid simple intuitive and impressionistic comments that are not grounded in language and do not draw on a viable set of analytical methods. For example, a recent review in the *Sunday Times* of Ann Enright's *The Green Road* (2016) remarked that the novel was 'brilliant, glittering fiction' and that 'her [Enright's] gaze is cool, her eye is lethal'. Although such comments might on the surface appear to form a valid analysis, it is actually very difficult to work out exactly what they mean. What, for example, does 'glittering' refer to in the context of discussing a literary work? And, to what extent is Enright's eye 'lethal'? If we ask these questions, it is easy to see that the comments tell us very little, if anything, about Enright's style. And, of course, 'glittering' and 'lethal' can mean different things to different groups of readers. As such, it is hard to pin down anything that can be explored with any reference to a principled set of tools and methods. These kinds of comments are essentially rhetorical and opaque rather than analytical and transparent.

As an antidote to this kind of approach, Paul Simpson (2014a) proposes that the practice of stylistics should conform to what he calls the 'three R's' so as to avoid this kind of intuitive response:

- Stylistic analysis should be rigorous
- Stylistic analysis should be retrievable
- Stylistic analysis should be replicable

(Simpson 2014a: 4)

Simpson argues that being *rigorous* means that the analysis is founded on an established and explicitly set-out method of analysis. In turn, being *retrievable* means that any analysis is grounded in a set of terms that are commonly shared and so allow others following the criticism to follow the argument and understand the language points that are being made. Finally, being *replicable* means that other stylisticians should be able to take the same method and apply it to a text so as to verify the approach taken and vouch for the credibility of an interpretation offered.

In this book, we encourage you to take Simpson's points seriously as you work with cognitive grammar and apply the model to texts both in the chapters that follow this one and beyond. As Simpson (2014a: 3) also notes, a fortunate empowering consequence of doing stylistics is that you will develop your understanding of the language system itself. Furthermore, stylistics offers the kind of principled parameters that make it possible to explicitly comment on the *how* of textual interpretation as well as the *what*, providing a way of what Stanley Fish (1980: 28) calls

> slow[ing] down the reading process so that events one does not notice in normal time but which do occur, are brought before our analytical attention. It is as if a slow-motion camera with an automatic stop action effect were recording our linguistic experiences and presenting them to us for viewing.

In this way, stylistics can be fully considered a discipline that integrates linguistic and literary study so as to bring to the surface the benefits of undertaking the analysis of texts through a linguistically informed lens.

Over time, stylisticians have become increasingly more interested in applying models from cognitive linguistics, including cognitive grammar, to their analyses of texts. This has resulted in the emergence of a subdiscipline, cognitive stylistics (or cognitive poetics), which has a strong grounding in cognitive linguistics while maintaining the methodology and central elements of good stylistic analysis (Simpson's three R's).

1.3 Grammar

Generally speaking, grammar refers both to the ways in which we structure language and how we talk about those structures. Perhaps, while not many of us would label ourselves as grammar specialists, grammar is nevertheless something that, as language users, we know about intuitively.

Any system of grammar – and there are many different 'grammars' – provides a description of how these units or structures work together, and the relationships between them. The majority of theories of grammar are premised on the idea of the **linguistic rank scale**. This rank scale describes how language can be structured hierarchically, starting with smaller units, such as morphemes, and how these smaller units can be combined in order to create larger units, such as clauses.

Consider, for example, how the following sentence is built up. We can make the word 'tomcat' from two different morphemes 'tom' and 'cat', and 'cat' is also a discrete lexical unit in its own right. Adding a definite article creates a phrase ('the tomcat'), and adding a verb, in turn, introduces an action of some kind which creates a clause, 'The tomcat sat', and so on. Here, we are simply stringing together smaller units of language to create a larger one.

Morpheme(s)	Tom + cat
Word	Tomcat
Phrase	The tomcat
Clause	The tomcat sat
Sentence	The tomcat sat on the mat

There are various ways that we can talk about the rules that govern these structures, and there have been a number of theories of grammar which have brought their own set of terms and ideas.

One of the most famous grammars is generative grammar. First developed by Noam Chomsky in the 1950s, generative grammar aims to both reveal principles about language that underpin all natural languages, and describe the laws that structure any given particular language. Generative grammar is further premised on the idea that all humans have an innate ability to process language and grammar, and, that consequently, we can describe some universal principles about how language is structured. While an influential model of grammar, generative grammar is not a favoured method of analysis in stylistics (see Fludernik 1994; Stockwell 2015). This is because it aims to represent a formal model of grammar that is independent from particular discourse contexts.

A grammar that does explore meaning in context, and from a less biologically oriented and more socially oriented perspective, is Michael Halliday's systemic-functional grammar. Systemic-functional grammar offers a systematic, user-friendly framework for text analysis that is centred on the exploration of interpretative effects – all of which makes it well suited for stylistic analyses. The grammar is largely based on Halliday's systemic grammar (1960s onwards), and has been revised and modified as stylistics has developed as a discipline. Systemic-functional grammar advocates that in language there is a

> set of options whereby the speaker encodes his or her experience of the processes of the external world, and of the internal world of his own consciousness, together with the participants in these processes and their attendant circumstances.

> (Halliday 1971: 119)

The idea of having a 'set of options' and choosing a particular way of representing a world experience has made systemic-functional grammar a highly useful model for exploring the representations of world view and ideology in texts, and systemic-functional grammar continues to be used for analysis in stylistics and in other areas of applied linguistics, such as critical discourse analysis (CDA). Furthermore, systems of grammar are not confined to text-based analysis. Kress and van Leeuwen's (1996) grammar of visual design, for example, takes ideas from systemic-functional grammar and adapts them to account for multimodal texts, namely posters and advertising.

1.4 What is 'cognitive grammar'?

Cognitive grammar is similar to systemic-functional grammar in that it also aims to explore how grammar is meaningful through usage-based analyses. Where cognitive grammar differs, however, is in its emphasis on cognition itself. Cognitive grammar[1] is a model of grammar that, along with other cognitive linguistic theories, asserts that all language is embodied. **Embodiment** refers to how our use and understanding of language is shaped by our physical experience in and with the world. Consequently, one of the key ideas underpinning cognitive grammar is that our conceptualizations – the way we, as producers of language, build and create meanings in our minds – are based on physical experiences, and that these in turn shape language. The rise in interest for the application of cognitive grammar for stylistics can be traced to the fact that the central ideas of cognitive grammar – the idea that language is premised on embodiment, and that any linguistic construction is meaningful – help us to address the concerns at the centre of stylistics as a practice: namely, the need to draw connections between textual patterns on the one hand and the interpretative and experiential responses of readers on the other.

This emphasis on experience and language as cognition means that the central concepts in cognitive grammar counter those put forward by generative grammar. Because of the fact it challenged Chomsky's views, when it was first developed in the late 1980s and early 1990s by Ronald Langacker, cognitive grammar was originally perceived as a radical model. As the field of cognitive linguistics has developed, however, and as the advances in cognitive stylistic analyses have similarly expanded, this reputation has somewhat altered.

Cognitive grammar is a type of construction grammar (see recommended further reading at the end of this chapter). A central idea that guides this group of grammars is that all uses of language are made up of symbolic units of form and meaning, called **constructions**. For example, a sentence like 'the tomcat sat on the mat' is a construction made up of discrete symbolic units. First, we have a string of concepts for which we have a mental model (e.g. we have a prototype (see Chapter 2) in our heads for what a tomcat should look like, what a mat should look like, and can imagine the act of sitting). Furthermore, we also have an embodied understanding of the spatial set-up of this scene. A preposition such as 'on', for example, similarly carries with it a mental template. We know that the tomcat sat on top of the mat, with the mat underneath, and so if asked to draw a representation of this sentence we would not situate the cat 'next' to, 'opposite' or 'under' the mat as we have a mental template about what this relationship – this image schema (see Chapter 2) – should look like. In this way, a symbolic unit as simple as the word 'on' carries important information about how we understand the spatial relationship in this sentence.

One of the most helpful aspects of talking about units of language in this way is that it allows us to move away from the idea of a grammar as following certain *rules*, and instead enables us to describe the relationship between lexicon and grammar in particular *usage events* (see Chapter 7). Further, the most distinctive part of this theory is the argument that all grammar is therefore inherently meaningful and 'it also reflects our basic experience of moving, perceiving and acting on the world' (Langacker 2008: 4–5). This reflection of basic experience accounts for how we can see the **principle of iconicity** operating in language. This idea pertains to the fact that there is a relationship between how we conceive things and how we express those conceptualizations in language. For example, we tend to describe our experiences in the order in which they occurred in time so that the grammatical structure mirrors the real-life event. This means that it would be usual to write 'I went to the shop and I bought some clothes' and unusual for the event to be presented as 'I bought some clothes and I went to the shop'. This principle can be seen operating at many different levels of grammar and is highlighted in many of the examples we draw on throughout this book.

1.5 Structure of book

This book is organized in the following way. Following this introduction, Chapters 2 through 7 each explore an important area of cognitive grammar. Each of these chapters begins with key objectives to guide your learning and introduces key content in a straightforward and accessible way. Main activities are provided throughout to check your understanding of the principles of cognitive grammar and its application to the stylistic analysis of texts. We have tried to include as many different examples of texts as possible in these activities both to show you the flexibility of cognitive grammar as an analytical tool, and to encourage you to explore a variety of discourse types. The chapters include texts as diverse as nineteenth-century poetry, multimodal advertising, government documentation, writing for children, television scripts and experimental contemporary literature.

At the end of each chapter, we provide a sample detailed analysis of an extract from a literary text. This analysis will model and apply the concepts and learning encountered in the chapter and will act as a springboard for you to develop expertise in working with cognitive grammar as you undertake your own stylistic analyses. As well as the main activities, there are further activities and suggestions for you to explore together with references to other valuable work in cognitive linguistics and cognitive stylistics which will act as a guide for further study. Finally, Chapter 8 provides a set of sample responses to all of the main text-based activities in this book, a set of additional extracts with questions, and some further areas for discussion that you may wish to explore. We also include short summaries of the key texts that we believe are particularly worth highlighting and which will provide you with a greater understanding of both theory and practice in the field.

On first mention, all key terms are highlighted in bold. Definitions of these terms can be found in the glossary at the end of the book.

1.6 Diagrams and illustrations

In his original work on cognitive grammar, Ronald Langacker uses diagrams extensively in order to help illustrate particular concepts. These diagrams are not meant to be formal representations of grammatical structures, but are instead, as Langacker (2008: 10) describes, intended to be 'heuristic' – a hands-on way of representing how we conceptualize units of language. These figures are typically made up of geometric shapes to symbolize linguistic concepts and relationships. If, for instance, you wanted to illustrate the spatial

Figure 1.1 Conceptualizing the spatial relationship of 'The tomcat sat on the mat'

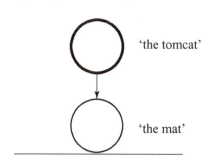

relationship in the above example of 'The tomcat sat on the mat', a typical cognitive grammar figure might be something as seen in Figure 1.1.

In Figure 1.1, 'the tomcat', as the subject of the sentence and the initiator of the action, holds more attention than the 'mat' and this is represented with a bold outline. As observed in Section 1.4, we have a mental template for the spatial relationship encoded through the preposition 'on' in the sentence, and this in turn is depicted by positioning 'the tomcat' above and 'the mat' below in this figure.

Throughout this book we also use a number of simple diagrams based on those of Langacker in addition to our own figures and illustrations. We do this as we believe that these visual representations help describe and explain grammatical phenomena. In each case, these are broken down and explained in the adjacent text.

1.7 Key sources and further reading

There are a number of very good books that introduce stylistics as an academic discipline. Simpson (2014a) is the best place to start for those looking for a detailed treatment with a strong pedagogical focus. Jeffries and McIntyre (2010) provide more advanced and technical coverage while more entry-level introductions can be found in Gregoriou (2009) and Giovanelli and Mason (2018). Gavins and Steen (2003) and Stockwell (2019) are essential reading for both an introduction to and wide-ranging coverage of cognitive poetics. Modern stylistics now embraces a wide range of different analytical methods and areas of analysis, including work in corpus stylistics, empirical reader response work and pedagogical applications in creative writing and the teaching of language and literature. Recently, several handbooks have been published that contain chapter-length discussions of these contemporary issues, concepts and approaches as well as overviews of the discipline's historical foundations: see Burke (2014); Stockwell and Whiteley (2014) and Sotirova (2015).

The key ideas for this book have been taken and adapted from a range of sources. The most succinct account of cognitive grammar is offered in Langacker (2008). Ideas have also been adapted from Taylor (2002), as well as other, more general cognitive linguistic sources, such as Croft and Cruse (2004), Evans and Green (2006) and Littlemore and Taylor (2014).

There have been a large number of publications on systemic-functional grammar. For the original accounts, see Halliday (1971, 1973, 1985); Halliday and Hasan (1976); Halliday and Matthiessen ([1985] 2013). For more on the ideas of visual grammar in multimodal contexts, see Kress and van Leeuwen (1996). If you are interested in comparing cognitive grammar further with other construction grammars, see Goldberg (1995), Kay and Fillmore (1999), Croft (2001) and Bergen and Chang (2005).

The very first application of cognitive grammar for stylistic analysis was carried out by Hamilton (2003). This chapter, which analyses Wilfred Owen's poem 'Hospital Barge', appeared in Gavins and Steen (2003).

Note

1. Please note that 'Cognitive Grammar' with capitals refers to the particular version of the theory put forward by Langacker, specifically. This book draws together wider ideas about the model, and therefore we refer to 'cognitive grammar' in lower case.

Chapter 2
Conceptual semantics

Key objectives

In this chapter we will explore:

- how cognitive grammar foregrounds the relationship between grammar and meaning;
- how we develop and use image schemas to structure concepts through language;
- how knowledge is encyclopaedic in so far as definitions of words are dynamic and based on use rather than fixed meanings;
- how larger areas of knowledge are stored in frames and domains; and
- how domains can be used to provide access to other parts of the same domain or another domain through metonymy and metaphor.

2.1 Grammar and meaning

As we saw in Chapter 1, one of the central tenets of cognitive grammar is that language itself is not an abstract system independent of other cognitive faculties but rather that it is inherently related to them. There is a meaningful relationship between how we experience the world and how we organize those experiences through language. Grammar in itself therefore carries meaning in that it inherently provides different ways (or construals – see Chapter 3) of presenting conceptual content, and of presenting and articulating meanings.

This chapter examines the basis of meaning behind grammatical forms by exploring some key ideas around the notion of meaning. In particular, we focus on cognitive grammar's central position that meaning resides in conceptualizations that arise in two ways. First, from the way we interact in the world with other people, and second, from the way we build and use knowledge which we draw on as part of these interactions.

2.2 Image schemas

One example of the way that the language we use is motivated by the physical and concrete world lies in the fact that we have a species-specific anatomy that influences the way that we view our environment and consequently the language we use to structure our experience. One very obvious and widely discussed example of this influence is the way that we use the front-back orientation of our bodies to project the notions of a 'front' and a 'back' onto objects. For example, we look ahead, generally move in a forward motion so that our own fronts move in the direction that we travel (nobody normally walks backwards for instance), and tend to communicate with other people face to face (it would be considered rude in many cultures to turn one's back on another person when talking to them). This sense of embodiment is mirrored in the way we spatially understand and conceptualize objects: we understand the front of stationary objects such as a computer screen as the side that faces us and, in Western culture, the front of a house is that which we can see from the public vantage point of a road or street rather than from the more private side that is usually in the back garden (see Figure 2.1). The physical world and the objects within that world therefore are understood through our embodied selves.

The templates that give rise to and structure concepts, and consequently the language we use to describe them, are known as image schemas. An **image schema** is a schematic representation of activity that is built up from our everyday sensory experiences (vision, touch, movement, force and balance) and through which we understand our conceptual world. In fact, a great

Figure 2.1 Conceptualizing objects as 'front' (left) and 'back' (right)

deal of research has demonstrated that image schemas derive from our first, early interactions with our physical environment as young infants where we develop understanding of sensory–perceptual aspects of vision, touch, motion and force as well as basic schemas such as containment, the movement of a path through space, the nature of up-down orientation and various kinds and degrees of interactional force.

It is important to remember that an image schema is not the same as a picture or a mental image. For example, it is very hard to draw an image schema in anything other than very basic terms (you can try this by attempting to draw 'balance' – it is actually quite difficult to do this in anything but a very abstract way). Although image schemas can be shown diagrammatically, the diagrams that are used are very skeletal and lack rich detail.

Image schemas that underpin spatial or locative relations are very common. For example, think about the preposition 'in' and a sentence such as 'the cat is in the garden'. In this instance, the relationship between the two entities relies on conceptualizing the garden as a bounded space within which the cat stands out: grammatically this lends itself to conventionally placing 'the cat' at the front of the clause. In this instance the cat is the prominent figure or **trajector** while the garden remains in the background as the **landmark** (see also the discussion of figure and ground in Chapter 3).

An example such as 'the cat is in the garden' also evokes a CONTAINMENT schema (small capital letters are used to denote an image schema). Figure 2.2 demonstrates its basic template of an inside and an outside separated by a boundary. This basic template has a specific internal logic that allows both physical and conceptual relationships to be expressed.

Figure 2.2 CONTAINMENT image schema

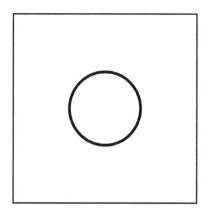

The relationship between the container (landmark) and its content (trajector) is grammatically marked by the use of prepositions such as 'in' and 'out'. This also provides a vehicle to conceptualize and talk about more abstract concepts which rely on a physical basis to give them meaning – for example, the idea of falling 'in' or 'out' of love – as in Text 2A, some very famous lines from William Shakespeare's *Romeo and Juliet*.

Text 2A

Romeo
Ah me! sad hours seem so long
Was that my father that went hence so fast?
Benvolio
It was: – What sadness lengthens Romeo's hours?
Romeo
Not having that, which having, makes them short
Benvolio
In love?
Romeo
Out –
Benvolio
Of love?
Romeo
Out of her favour where I am in love

(*RJ* 1.1.161–68)

In this exchange Romeo and Benvolio draw on the spatial relations enacted by the prepositions 'in' and 'out' using their physical bases as a way of providing a structure for the more complex abstract concepts of love and favour. In these instances, being 'in' the marked boundary of a state (here Romeo having his admiration for his first love in the play, Rosalind, reciprocated) is seen in positive terms while the converse side of the CONTAINMENT image schema, 'out', marks Romeo as trajector removed and at a distance from Rosalind as landmark and is viewed in negative terms. These basic but powerful notions of 'in' and 'out' permeate the entire play, of course, and form an important part of the characters' identities: for example, when Romeo and Juliet fall 'in' love, the dynamics of the play change to precipitate the tragedy of their deaths. We will return to image schemas and their relationship to metaphor in Section 2.4.3.

Another very common image schema derives from the experience of our body moving through space and time from an initial to an ending point. A SOURCE-PATH-GOAL schema also has its own inherent spatial logic: In this instance the trajector moves from a starting point or **source** along a **path**

Figure 2.3 SOURCE-PATH-GOAL image schema

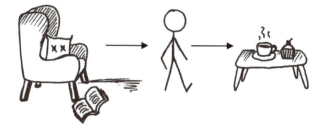

towards an intended destination point or **goal**. At any given time, the trajector may be moving in a particular way and may be at a certain distance from the goal. Equally, the final resting place of the trajector may or may not be the intended goal, and obstacles and detours might be imagined to take the trajector away from its path either temporarily or permanently.

As with CONTAINMENT, the SOURCE-PATH-GOAL image-schema is derived from the ways in which our own bodies move in the physical world, and provides a template for conceptualizing the meaning of concepts expressed by prepositions such as 'toward', 'away', and 'along', all of which denote the movement of a trajector away from a landmark along a given path. For example:

1   She (trajector) walked towards the table (landmark)

2   She (trajector) moved away from the chair (landmark)

3   She (trajector) shifted along the side of the table (landmark)

In each of these instances, there is an inherent SOURCE-PATH-GOAL image schema. In example 1, the source is unspecified but extends along the path towards the goal of the table. In example 2, the source is now specified but the goal remains undetermined. And in example 3, both the source and the goal remain unspecified, with the path being made more explicit. Together these examples demonstrate variations of a more basic or central SOURCE-PATH-GOAL template.

These types of **elaboration** are also present within an image schema represented by a single preposition. The preposition 'out' has as its central schema a trajector moving out from within the landmark so that the two are completely discrete entities, as in 'she walked out of the room'. The following two examples, however, show uses of 'out' that highlight different relationships between the trajector and landmark.

- He pulled the plant out of its pot (only part of the trajector is initially in the landmark)

- She took out two books from the library (the trajector is part of a larger group that is the landmark)

Finally, many image schemas occur as part of a larger overarching group. For example, a FORCE image schema has several separate schemas: compulsion, blockage, enablement, removal of restraint and so on (see Chapter 6 for more on FORCE in the discussion of cognitive grammar's treatment of modality).

Activity 2.1: Exploring image schemas

Read Text 2B, the opening to Ian McEwan's *Nutshell*. Very unusually, the narrator in this case is an unborn baby still in his mother's womb.

Text 2B

So here I am, upside down in a woman. Arms patiently crossed, waiting, waiting and wondering who I'm in, what I'm in for. My eyes close nostalgically when I remember how I once drifted in my translucent body bag, floated dreamily in the bubble of my thoughts through my private ocean in slow-motion somersaults, colliding gently against the transparent bounds of my confinement, the confiding membrane that vibrated with, even as it muffled, the voices of conspirators in a vile enterprise. That was in my careless youth. Now, fully inverted, not an inch of space to myself, knees crammed against belly, my thoughts as well as my head are fully engaged. I've no choice, my ear is pressed all day and night against the bloody walls. I listen, make mental notes, and I'm troubled. I'm hearing pillow talk of deadly intent and I'm terrified by what awaits me, by what might draw me in.

(McEwan 2017: 1)

1 To what extent does this extract draw on image schemas to help shape meaning?

2 What do you think is the effect of such image schemas?

2.3 Encyclopaedic semantics and categorization

2.3.1 Dictionary versus encyclopaedic view of meaning

The question of what individual words actually mean is an important one in cognitive grammar. To answer this involves examining the very nature of what meaning is. A traditional view is that a word's meaning is simply the information contained in its dictionary definition. Unsurprisingly, this is known as the **dictionary view of meaning**. In this view, the definition of a word exists independently of any real-world or contextual knowledge relating to how a word is actually used. So, for example, the word 'car' simply means a vehicle with four wheels, powered by an engine and able to carry passengers. However, the dictionary view does not account for meanings associated with how cars are driven or what they feel like to drive, nor does it capture any experiential knowledge that an individual might have, for example, about the car that their parents had when they were younger or when they first learnt to drive. Knowledge of this type would be considered nonlinguistic and not relevant to a discussion of meaning.

From a cognitive linguistic perspective, however, this view is highly problematic in that it treats meaning as distinct from cultural knowledge and experience and draws a line between the study of semantics (word meaning) and pragmatics (meanings in context). Such a view suggests words can be defined and understood outside of the contexts in which they are used. In contrast, cognitive approaches to language propose an **encyclopaedic view of meaning** that captures more clearly how a word's definition is related to the ways in which it is used which may be personal and/or shared and also culturally specific. In this view, words act as points of access to a store of encyclopaedic knowledge of different types. This knowledge is dynamic in that it changes through time as we continually experience and interact in our social world. Some of this knowledge is more central in that it is always activated when a word is used, while other knowledge is less central and only activated in certain contexts. For example, in the UK, the knowledge an individual might have that cars can be used to drive along roads would be highly central to the definition of a car. However, the knowledge that they once broke down driving to London, although part of experiential, encyclopaedic knowledge, is less central and would most likely only be activated in specific contexts, for example, when talking about bad motoring experiences.

2.3.2 Categories and prototypes

We make sense of the world by making connections between aspects of our experience. As we have seen above, this can relate to how we build up rich encyclopaedic stores of knowledge that are accessed through the use of particular words. In this section, we will look at how we build up knowledge through assigning concepts to a **category**.

Take a category such as 'sports' whose membership is usually composed of largely physical activities that are played competitively either individually or as teams. This category has various members all with different degrees of membership. For example, in the UK, 'football' would appear to be a very

Figure 2.4 The 'sports' category

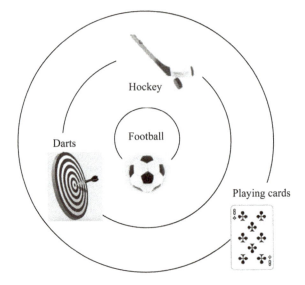

good example of a sport, as would 'hockey', although arguably due to its relatively lower popularity, it would be a less good example. Alternatively, 'darts' while being something that is played competitively and is on television sports channels feels intuitively less sport-like, perhaps due to the perception that it is not an overly physical game. And, for most people, despite 'playing cards' being something that is played in a competitive way, it is likely to be viewed as bad example of a sport if at all.

Category membership can therefore be viewed in terms of **gradience** with a central member or **prototype** and non-prototypical members of varying degrees. This can be seen in the radial structure shown in Figure 2.4. At the edge is the peripheral member, 'playing cards'.

It is important to remember that the degree to which an object sits in relation to a category is to a very large extent culturally dependent. Imagine, for example, that you visit a friend of yours who lives in the United States. In that culture, 'basketball', 'American football', 'baseball' and 'ice hockey' are much more likely to be perceived as central members of the category 'sport'.

The notions category membership and prototypes can be applied to stylistic analysis in a number of ways. For example, at the level of the sentence, we can say that there is a prototype that contains a finite verb: in some grammars, having a finite verb is essential. Some sentences, however, are clearly more peripheral. For example, look at Text 2C, an extract from Susan Hill's *The Mist in the Mirror*.

Text 2C

> Rain, rain all day, all evening, all night, pouring autumn rain. Out on the
> country, over field and fen and moorland, sweet-smelling rain, borne on the
> wind. Rain in London, rolling along gutters, gurgling down drains. Street
> lamps blurred by rain. A policeman walking by in a cape, rain gleaming silver
> on its shoulders. Rain bouncing on roofs and pavements, soft rain falling
> secretly in woodland and on dark heath. Rain on London's river, and slanting
> among the sheds, wharves and quays. Rain on suburban gardens, dense with
> laurel and rhododendron. Rain from north to south and from east to west, as
> though it had never rained until now, and now might never stop.
>
> (Hill 1992: 9)

In this extract, no finite verbs appear until the final line. Instead, the verb
forms: 'pouring', 'borne', 'rolling along', 'blurred', 'walking by', 'gleam-
ing', 'bouncing', 'falling' and 'slanting' are all non-finite participial forms
that give the impression that we, as readers, are close to the action, which
seems to be ongoing with no real sense of beginning or end. It would be
wrong, however, to say that this extract does not contain any sentences; rather,
the sentences are not prototypical ones and consequently give rise to certain
interpretative effects (see also Chapter 5 on scanning).

At the extreme end, some sentences, usually called minor sentences, may
have no verb at all. This is the case in a further section, Text 2D, from *The
Mist in the Mirror*.

Text 2D

> Rain on all the silent streets and squares, alleys and courts, gardens and
> churchyards and stone steps and nooks and crannies of the city.
> Rain. London. The back end of the year.
>
> (Hill 1992: 2)

In this extract, there is a distinct absence of verbs. Since verbs show processes
through time (see Chapter 5), the effect of the chain of noun phrases is arguably to continue to emphasize the timeless picture of the scene, evident in the
string of three noun phrases in the final line: the nouns 'rain' and 'London',
which are repeated from the earlier description and the final noun phrase
incorporating a prepositional phrase 'The back end of the year'.

Finally, we can use the notion of the prototype to account for the idea
of foregrounding. Foregrounding involves either the setting up of patterns
across lexical, phonological or grammatical structures (parallelism) or the
breaking of patterns (deviation) with interpretative effects. Here are the first
two lines of Carol Ann Duffy's poem 'Valentine'.

Text 2E

Not a red rose or a satin heart.
I give you an onion

(Duffy 1993)

The beginning of this poem relies on a reader understanding the disconnect between the category 'Valentine's gifts' and the 'onion' that Duffy's speaker presents to her lover. In this instance, the fact that an 'onion' would typically be a very bad example of a Valentine's gift results in strong deviation from an expected norm; the peripheral (if at all) member 'onion' foregrounds the unconventional way in which love and relationships are represented at the beginning of the poem.

Activity 2.2: Prototypes and deviation in poetry

1   Find 'Valentine' (easily available online) and explore how this initial deviation works to set up the remainder of the poem.

2   You could also find poems of your own that rely on a similar disconnect between a given category and our expectations of membership of that category for effect. Can you explain how such a practice works in terms of providing a striking image and rich interpretative effects?

2.4 Frames and domains

2.4.1 Frames

In Section 2.3.1 we examined the encyclopaedic view of knowledge and explored how we store our understanding and experiences of the world. Thus, it was argued that our knowledge of the category 'car' includes the various types of knowledge about cars that we have both experienced directly and read and heard about indirectly. Together this bundle of knowledge is known as a schema or **frame**. So, we also have a 'restaurant' frame, a 'supermarket' frame and a 'university library' frame, all of which contain the various kinds of knowledge that we need to help us when we want to order something to eat, go shopping or do some research. Furthermore, we have frames that contain knowledge of books and films. For example, a reader might have a *Frankenstein* frame that contains all of their knowledge of the plot and characters, the author Mary Shelley, the responses of literary critics to the novel, the story behind its composition, its influence on gothic and science-fiction literature in the two hundred years since it was written, its appropriation into mainstream popular culture and so on. Some of this information might have been acquired second-hand from talking and reading about the book and from integrating other people's thoughts into the *Frankenstein* frame. For some books, a frame is built up entirely from this kind of second-hand experience. For example, neither of us has read Charles Dickens' *The Old Curiosity Shop* but we have read literary criticism and reviews of the novel, heard people talking about it and feel that we both know its plot and two of its most famous characters, Little Nell and Daniel Quilp, pretty well.

2.4.2 Domains

Although sometimes used interchangeably with frame, a **domain** is a wider, more general area of knowledge and is used more explicitly in cognitive grammar. A domain provides background information against which specific words are both understood and used. For example, the words 'arm', 'hand' and 'finger' are all from the domain of 'body'. We need to have access to knowledge in this domain to understand and use these words. In doing so, we place the words as salient, foregrounded lexical items against the background of the entire domain, so that when we use the word 'hand' we usually understand it to be part of a body (see also Chapter 3, Section 3.3.1 on scope and Section 3.3.3 on figure and ground).

Activity 2.3: Domains in poetry

Read Text 2F, 'This living hand', a poem by John Keats.

Text 2F

This living hand, now warm and capable
Of earnest grasping, would, if it were cold
And in the icy silence of the tomb,
So haunt thy days and chill thy dreaming nights
That thou would wish thine own heart dry of blood
So in my veins red life might stream again,
And thou be conscience-calm'd – see here it is –
I hold it towards you.

(Keats 1898)

1 Comment on any words (or groups of words) that you think are significant in the poem and the domains that they evoke?

2 How does your knowledge of these domains affect your understanding of the poem?

Generally, a word or expression will evoke several domains, known as a **domain matrix**. For example, our knowledge about the word 'glass' as in the expression 'a glass of orange juice' includes its shape and size, its use to store a liquid and drink out of it, the fact that it can be smashed if dropped, can be washed and used again and so on. The understanding of this single word is thus drawn from a variety of domains: physical object, space, function, material and size.

2.4.3 Metaphor

Domains are also commonly used as access points to other domains. Writers and speakers often explain ideas by drawing on knowledge from one domain to provide a structure for understanding a second one. For example, read the following expressions, all of which might be said by someone talking about their life.

● I started off working in the city and I'll probably end up there too

● I feel like I've reached a dead end

● It's time for me to move on

In each case, one domain (life) is given structure and meaning in terms of another domain (journey). A journey is something tangible that we directly encounter in the physical world and so this process of structuring has a strong experiential basis. In this instance, the knowledge and experience that speakers have of a journey is used to give structure and meaning to the more abstract concept of life. This gives rise to the **conceptual metaphor** of LIFE IS A JOURNEY (in conventional conceptual metaphor notation, small capital letters and a X IS Y structure are used).

The process by which these two domains are connected is known as **mapping**. Mapping takes place as a result of the **source domain** providing structure to the **target domain**. In LIFE IS A JOURNEY, aspects of the source domain 'journey' are mapped across to provide structure to corresponding aspects in the target domain as shown in Table 2.1.

It is no coincidence that in the case of LIFE IS A JOURNEY, the source domain is a concrete area of knowledge while the target domain is an abstract one. In fact, conceptual metaphors operate precisely because there are domains of abstract knowledge to which we have no real access and consequently need interpreting and repackaging in physical terms. Thus, we use our experience

Table 2.1 Mappings in LIFE IS A JOURNEY, from Giovanelli (2014b)

Travellers	⟶	People
Starting point	⟶	Birth
End point	⟶	Death
Events and actions experienced, and places visited	⟶	Episodes in life
Distance travelled	⟶	Progress in career, relationships, etc.
Deciding on a route	⟶	Making life choices
Obstacles on a journey		Problems in life to overcome

of the physical world and those concrete areas of knowledge to provide a structure and a set of concepts through which abstract ideas, feelings and concepts can be understood and communicated. Importantly, the conditions or context in which individuals write or speak influence or constrain the source domains that are likely to be selected and used. For example, read Text 2G, taken from a report on a postponed football match in 2013.

Text 2G

Northern Ireland's World Cup qualifier against Russia has fallen foul of the weather for the second time in 24 hours, with hostile conditions rendering Windsor Park unplayable

> http://www.independent.co.uk/sport/football/news-and-comment/football-matches-called-off-due-to-poor-weather-as-rain-and-snow-batters-england-8546802.html

In this example, the expression 'hostile weather' is a realization of the metaphor THE WEATHER IS A MENACING PERSON. The target domain 'weather' is given structure via the domain of knowledge associated with an uncooperative and dangerous person. The journalist's choice of source domain to structure his representation of the event is likely to have been influenced by the physical setting itself and the experience of feeling 'under attack' from the rain and snow. Some additional common source and target domains are shown in Table 2.2.

Because they are derived from sensory experience, image schemas (discussed in Section 2.1) make very good source domains. For example, the image schemas UP-DOWN, IN-OUT and FRONT-BACK, all of which arise from

Table 2.2 Common source and target domains, from Kövecses (2010: 17–31)

Common source domains	Common target domains
the human body; health and illness; animals; plants; buildings and constructions; machines and tools; games and sport; business transactions; cooking and food; heat and cold; light and darkness; forces; movement and direction	emotion; desire; morality; thought; society; politics; the economy; human relationships; communication; time; life and death; religion; events and actions

the ways in which our bodies interact and are consequently inherently meaningful, give rise to a number of **orientational metaphors**. For example, look at Text 2H, part of a speech by the UK Chancellor of Exchequer, Philip Hammond in March 2017.

Text 2H

Last year, the British economy grew faster than the United States, faster than Japan, faster than France

Indeed amongst the major advanced economies Britain's growth in 2016 was second only to Germany

Employment is at a record high. Unemployment is at an 11 year low, with over 2.7 million more people enjoying the security and dignity of work than in 2010.

https://www.gov.uk/government/speeches/spring-budget-2017-philip-hammonds-speech

In this extract, the UP-DOWN image schema provides the source domain for the conceptual metaphor UP IS GOOD, which is informed by one's own experiential understanding of physical aspects, such as the fact that living things tend to grow upwards. This metaphor is realized in the phrase 'the British economy grew', 'Britain's growth' and 'employment is at a record high'. A SOURCE-PATH-GOAL image schema also underpins the growth metaphor: we understand that things grow from a starting point along a path, here of course a (metaphorical) vertical one.

Activity 2.4: Metaphor in advertising

Advertising is a genre that often makes extensive use of metaphor to fulfil its purpose of informing potential customers about a product or service and persuading them to buy it. Generally, metaphors in advertising discourse are used both to draw attention to the product or service being advertised in a striking and original way often using an image to do so, and to present favourable analogies between other concepts or objects that have the characteristics that the advertiser wants to associate with their product.

Read Text 2I, a multimodal (uses an image as well as words) advertisement for a professional training course aimed at business leaders.

Text 2I: Advertisement for a professional training course

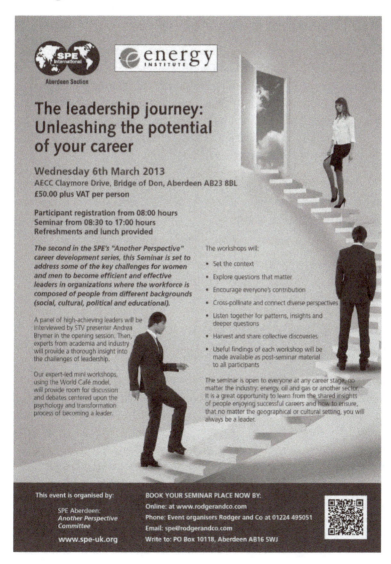

How does this advertisement draw on metaphors to help support the message that it wishes to convey?

2.4.4 Metonymy

Whereas metaphor involves a mapping between domains, metonymy (see also Section 4.5.3) is a process whereby mapping occurs between two entities in the same domain so that one stands for the other. A frequently quoted example of this is in the sentence below, spoken by one server to another in a café.

- The ham sandwich is waiting for his bill

In this instance, the expression 'ham sandwich' refers to a customer in the café rather than the sandwich itself and acts as the vehicle to allow access to the target concept, the customer, who is part of the same café domain. Within this context, the server's use of 'ham sandwich' rather than simply 'the customer' could well be motivated by the fact that 'ham sandwich' is an easier way of highlighting exactly which customer is being referred to.

Common types of metonymy include:

- PART FOR WHOLE: My wheels are parked outside (wheels = car);
- WHOLE FOR PART: England won the World Cup in 1966 (England = England's football team);
- PRODUCER FOR PRODUCT: I've bought a new VW (VW = car);
- PLACE FOR INSTITUTION: Downing Street announces honours list (Downing Street = British government).

2.5 Extended analysis

The following section draws together the ideas and concepts covered in this chapter in an example analysis of Text 2J, the opening to Stella Gibbons' short story 'Roaring tower'. The narrator is a nineteen-year-old woman whose parents have forced her to end a relationship and have sent her away from London to stay with some relatives in Cornwall. This extract describes Clara getting into a train compartment and leaving her mother and father.

Text 2J

My father bent his head to kiss me, but I turned my face away and his lips brushed the edge of my veil instead. Over his shoulder I met my mother's grieved eyes, and my own filled with tears.

I lowered my veil, with trembling fingers, murmured some words which I have now forgotten, and stepped into the compartment, my father holding the door open for me. On the seat in the corner lay a bunch of white roses, a copy of a ladies' journal, and a basket packed with refreshment for the journey.

My heart was like stone. The roses, picked from the garden of our house in Islington, softened if not a whit. I moved them aside carefully and sank into my corner seat. I said not a word; and my father and mother stood in silence too; how I wished they would go away!

'You will write tomorrow, my child, and tell us what your journey was like and how your Aunt Julia is?' said my mother.

'Yes, Mamma.' My lips felt stiff and cold.

'Remember, Clara, we shall expect you to take full advantage of the Cornish air, and return to us in a very different frame of mind and quite respired to health.' My father's voice was a warning.

'Yes, Papa.'

I folded my black-gloved hands on my lap, and stared out of the window, avoiding my mother's eyes.

(Gibbons 1937: 1)

A useful place to start with any analysis is to outline your initial interpretations and then work backwards to explain explicitly how the language in the text gives rise to your reading. One common interpretation of the opening of this text is that there is tension between Clara and her parents: she turns away from her father's kiss, trembles, describes her sadness and wishes her parents would leave her alone. In turn, Clara's father speaks in a warning tone as she leaves, and the extract ends with her avoiding her mother's eye, presumably as the train is about to leave. With this in mind, it is now possible to start to map out some of the language features of the text.

One of the prominent aspects of the text is the number of elaborations of SOURCE-PATH-GOAL and CONTAINMENT image schemas. In the first paragraph, there is a series of movements that describe both the actions of Clara and her family and also allow us to infer aspects of their relationship. Initially, the father's head (the trajector) moves downwards but does not reach its goal (kissing his daughter) since Clara turns her face away. Here then, the trajector rests on the periphery of the landmark ('brushed the edge of my veil instead') rather than reaching its goal of the kiss. A prepositional phrase, 'Over his shoulder', introduces another elaboration of the SOURCE-PATH-GOAL schema: in this instance, two trajectors each move along a path to meet in the middle as Clara's eyes make contact with her mother's.

In this paragraph, Clara's narration also draws on a CONTAINMENT image schema, 'my own eyes filled with tears'. Indeed, as we will see later in the analysis, the notion of being 'inside' something else is an important motif and thematic concern. In this instance, the trajector (Clara's 'tears') fills up her eyes; she is of course, in love and in pain. This sense of unhappiness is heightened through the domain from which the paragraph draws: words like 'veil' and 'grieved' are suggestive of a state of mourning (in fact throughout the remainder of the story, Clara treats the loss of her lover more like a death than a separation).

In the second paragraph, there is a further example of the SOURCE-PATH-GOAL image schema denoting movement as Clara lowers her veil; interestingly, the sense of downwards movement is echoed in the choice of the speech verb 'murmurs', which suggests low volume. Arguably these choices also cohere with the overall sense of grief and loss, additionally demonstrated in the fact that the narrator can no longer remember her words at the time. The second paragraph also contains various elaborations of the basic CONTAINMENT image schema. So, there is the sense of movement as Clara (the trajector) moves to rest inside the train compartment (landmark); in this instance, the phrasal verb 'stepped into' also is underpinned by the SOURCE-PATH-GOAL image schema. Additionally, two embedded prepositional phrases, 'on the seat' and 'in the corner' and the past participle 'packed' express near-containment or containment relationships.

The third paragraph begins with an analogy 'my heart was like stone', which again can be read as cohering with the sense of grief and loss, and possibly downwards movement or even stasis (stone is of considerable weight). Further examples of SOURCE-PATH-GOAL and CONTAINMENT schemas can be found underpinning various descriptions. The roses (trajector) are first described as displaced from the ground (landmark) through the act of being picked from Clara's garden, and then moved across from one part of the train seat to another to allow Clara to sit down. Clara's own movement here follows a vertical downwards path towards containment as she (trajector) 'sank' into her 'corner seat' (landmark). There are also explicit markers of emptiness and further indicators of stasis, both mental/internal through the use of the negation 'said not a word' and 'in silence', and physical since Clara's father and mother are described using the verb 'stood', which denotes a lack of movement. Furthermore, Clara's desire that they 'would go away' expresses another instantiation of the SOURCE-PATH-GOAL IMAGE schema and provides a powerful contrast to the earlier stasis; in this instance, the inability of the family to say anything to each other about the situation is in opposition to Clara's own internal wish for separation. Ironically, out of duty and respect she is unable to explicitly articulate these thoughts and, tragically, the movement away from her parents echoes – or perhaps is a response to – her lover being forced to leave her. When she does speak, she is able to utter only pairs of words, 'Yes, Mamma' and 'Yes, Papa'. In her first response, she is barely able to speak; her 'stiff and cold lips' draw further on the sense of stasis, grief and loss.

The remainder of the extract draws explicitly on the notion of a journey with a SOURCE-PATH-GOAL image schema functioning as the source domain in the conceptual metaphor LIFE IS A JOURNEY. This is evident in the sense that Clara is being asked by her parents to move on with her life; they view the physical train journey she is taking as a necessary and quite natural stage to allow Clara to get over and lose the memory of her lover and to 'return … in a very different state of mind and quite respired to health'. Indeed, the highlighting of movement away from one part of a life into another and the sense of self-discovery and later reflection (we learn that Clara is recounting the narrative events from fifty years in the future) are important concerns of the story as it progresses.

At the end of the extract, the closing image schema of movement is evident in the folding of Clara's hands 'on my lap' (the hands as trajector come to rest on the landmark) and her staring 'out of the window' (the goal here is exists explicitly beyond and avoiding her mother). This final image of movement away from, rather than towards, her parents highlights the distance and sense of anger that Clara feels and yet, is unable to explicitly articulate. Instead of words, Clara's movements, actions (or lack of them) and internalized thought processes convey her sense of isolation. Her lack of agency regarding decisions about her own life and her subservience to her parents' wishes manifest themselves in a series of patterns built around containment and various kinds of movement.

Finally, and as indicated throughout, the extract draws on various domains to provide coherence and foreground some key thematic concerns. These are namely the domains of love, journeys, emotions and honour and, together with grammatical patterns, they act to foreground specific ideas that have been discussed in this analysis. Of course, the comments here represent just one possible set of features and interpretations and you may well have identified and explored other possible patterns in language and consequent readings of this extract. You could also read the remainder of the story to see how far the points raised here and/or in your own analysis can be examined in more detail and developed.

2.6 Further activities

1.

Read Text 2K, the poem 'Love's Philosophy', by Percy Bysshe Shelley.

Text 2K

The fountains mingle with the river
    And the rivers with the ocean,
The winds of heaven mix for ever
    With a sweet emotion;
Nothing in the world is single;
    All things by a law divine
In one spirit meet and mingle.
    Why not I with thine? –

See the mountains kiss high heaven
    And the waves clasp one another;
No sister-flower would be forgiven
    If it disdained its brother;
And the sunlight clasps the earth
    And the moonbeams kiss the sea:
What is all this sweet work worth
    If thou kiss not me?

(Shelley [1819] 2002: 409)

Comment on any language features what you find significant and interesting in the light of your work in this chapter. You could include, where relevant, your thoughts on how the language of the poem can be explored in terms of:

- image schemas
- categories, frames and domains
- metaphor

2.

Find your own examples of political speeches and or advertising that you think make interesting use of metaphor and/or metonymy. Can you analyse these in terms of the cross or within-domain mappings that occur? How do these mappings work to create meanings in the texts that you have chosen?

3.

Take one of the concepts from any of the sections in this chapter and undertake some wider reading using the 'Further reading' suggestions below as a starting point. To what extent do you think the concept you have explored supports you in undertaking stylistic analyses of texts? What do you think are the benefits of using this particular concept and what might be its limitations?

2.7 Further reading

A summary of the relationship between conceptual semantics and cognitive grammar can be found in Chapter 2 of Langacker (2008). Good coverage generally of embodied cognition and the experiential basis of meaning is in Lakoff and Johnson (1999), Evans and Green (2006) and Giovanelli (2014b). Image schemas are examined in detail in Johnson (1987), Hampe (2005) and Ungerer and Schmid (2006). Mandler (2004) gives an intriguing account of how image schemas support the development of thought and speech in young children and offer meaningful structures into which new knowledge is assimilated. There are also detailed sections on image schemas in Lakoff (1987), Gibbs and Colston (1995) and Evans and Green (2006). The notion of categories is briefly summarized in Chapter 1 of Radden and Dirven (2007) and given extensive treatment in Rosch (1975, 1978), Lakoff (1987) and Ungerer and Schmid (2006). The notion of a frame is from Fillmore (1985). The idea of a narrative schema is explained in Mason (2014). Chapter 4 of Langacker (1987) discusses the concept of a domain in cognitive grammar, which is also outlined in Chapter 22 of Taylor (2002) and Chapter 2 of Langacker (2008). Some classic texts for metaphor (and metonymy) are Lakoff and Johnson (1980), Lakoff and Turner (1989), Turner (1998), Kövecses (2005, 2006, 2010, 2015) and Semino (2008). An alternative way of viewing metaphor as a *conceptual blend* is discussed and developed in Fauconnier and Turner (2002). Stockwell (2002) provides clear overviews, together with exemplary stylistic analyses, of all the sections covered in this chapter. There has been a range of work in stylistics on the topics covered in this chapter. For good overviews, see Jeffries and McIntyre (2010) and Stockwell (2019). More specifically, interesting explorations of metaphor in advertising (including aspects of multimodality) can be found in Semino (2008), Koller (2009), Hidalgo-Downing, Kraljevic-Mujic and Núñez Perucha (2013) and Hidalgo-Downing and Kralijevic-Mujic (2011). Specific treatment of metaphor within the cognitive grammar framework can be found in Browse (2014, 2016) and Päivärinta (2014). A chapter-length analysis of Keats' 'This living hand' from a cognitive stylistic perspective is in Giovanelli (2013).

Chapter 3
Construal

Key objectives

In this chapter we will explore:

- the notion of construal in cognitive grammar;
- how cognitive grammar distinguishes between different dimensions of construal; and
- how the ways in which writers and speakers construe events form important patterns in clauses and longer stretches of text.

3.1 An introduction to construal

Construal is an important concept in cognitive grammar. As we have indicated in Chapter 2, one of cognitive grammar's central claims is that the meaning of an expression exists simply not in the conceptual content it evokes but also relies on how that content is presented.

As an example, imagine walking through a park at the same time a football match is taking place. Looking onto the pitch, you could refer to the people playing the sport in any number of different ways, including

- footballers,
- a team,
- people running about kicking a ball.

These examples demonstrate how language provides us with the means to offer alternative construals of the same scene. In the first example, we could draw on our knowledge of the sport to specifically provide a name for the players. And, in the second and third, we could choose a different construal either to represent the concept of a group as a distinctive coherent whole 'a team', or to highlight the multiple participants within it, 'people running about kicking a ball'.

Another visual analogy may be helpful in understanding how construal works. Imagine a theatre stage with actors on it and props such as chairs and tables. In the context of a performance, a director is able to position these items in certain ways so as to create meaning for the audience – for example, placing one actor at the front of the stage or sitting at a table to show a particular power relationship and so on. Equally, the position of the audience may well affect the way they interpret the scene and the meaning they attach to it. For example, sitting at the front or the back or to one particular side affords a slightly different perspective of the events on the stage. The shaping of material and the positioning of those receiving it thus form an integral part of the meaning-making process.

Figure 3.1 shows the relationship between the two **conceptualizers** of a construal (i.e. the speaker/writer and hearer/reader) and the **conceived scene**. The lower level of the figure including the conceptualizers is known as the **ground**, which is the context within which any form of communication takes place.

The visual analogy is a useful one for cognitive grammar since construal is intuitively very similar to how visual perception operates. And, as we will see in the remainder of this chapter, it can be very fruitful to think of the different dimensions of construal in visual terms. In this chapter, we will focus on the following three dimensions of construal:

- Specificity: how closely we choose to view a scene or parts of it;
- Focus and prominence: what we choose to look at and pay attention to within in the scene; and
- Perspective: the position from which we view a scene.

The study of specificity and focus/prominence are concerned with how the conceived scene is presented (the horizontal level indicated by the bold line in Figure 3.1), while perspective is concerned with how the conceptualizers

Figure 3.1 The construal relationship (after Verhagen 2007)

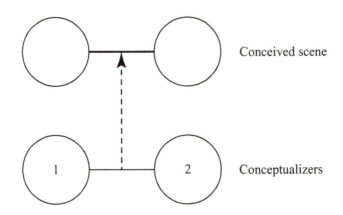

are positioned in relation to the conceived scene (the vertical level indicated by the dashed line).

In the remainder of this chapter, we will work through each of these dimensions in turn.

3.2 Specificity

One of the ways that we use language is to emphasize degrees of **specificity** by zooming in or out on a particular scene. For example, if you walk into a market, you might see a range of different types of fruit on a stall there. You could construe what you see in a number of different ways. You might use the term 'fruit' which, in itself, is a fairly general term that gives us enough information to be able to understand the broader category but does not discriminate between the different types of fruit that might be on the stall. On the other hand, we can zoom in to talk about 'apples', 'oranges', 'bananas' and so on, and each of these terms provides a greater degree of specificity. Indeed the zooming analogy is used in cognitive grammar to describe how more specific terms give us greater **granularity** and less specific ones greater **generality**.

Of course, it is possible to increase the granularity by construing the scene in an even more specific way. For example, you might want to mention the fact that the apple is 'green' or 'red', is 'small' or 'large' or is a particular variety, for example, a 'Granny Smith' or a 'Golden Delicious'. Each choice adds a greater granularity to the description. Maintaining the visual analogy, increasing the resolution allows finer details to become foregrounded, while more general ones remain in the background.

The relationship between 'fruit' and the various more specific choices is handled by cognitive grammar's notion of **elaboration**. In British English, the more schematic term 'fruit' may be elaborated or extended to form a chain where each subsequent part of the chain is relatively more specific than the one that precedes it.

In fact in the chain in Figure 3.2, the more schematic term 'fruit' categorizes all examples of the ones that follow. The elaboration chain also helps us understand why some construals might be used in some contexts but not in others. For example, imagine being at the market and wanting to buy some apples. In this instance, the schematic term 'fruit' is clearly not going to be

Figure 3.2 Elaboration of 'fruit'

fruit → apple → green apple → large green apple → large green Granny Smith apple

Figure 3.3 Elaborative relations

> Something happened → Joanne Smith suffers injury → Joanne Smith has hurt her foot → Joanne Smith has broken her calcaneus bone

of much use, whereas the various elaborations will be much more useful depending on what you wish to buy and the degree of choice the market holder is offering; if you simply want some green apples then you will not need to use one of the final two terms at the right-hand end of the chain.

This notion of an **elaborative relation** can be scaled up to account for larger, more novel structures. For example, imagine reporting on a professional sportswoman suffering an injury before a big tournament. A chain showing successive elaborative relations could be represented as in Figure 3.3.

Importantly, it is the context that determines the degree of specificity that a speaker or writer is likely to use in any given situation. 'Something happened' is so general as to be of little real use but 'suffers injury' is at a general enough level to give us sufficient information. In contrast, 'has hurt her foot' adds a greater layer of granularity to allow a listener or reader access to what has specifically happened, while 'has broken her calcaneus bone' offers a finer granularity that would probably only be needed by medical professionals. In each of these cases, the way that the event is construed depends on how much detail is required in that particular context.

Activity 3.1: Exploring the effects of specificity in the ghost genre

Look at Text 3A. This is an extract from a short story, 'The Inn at Shillingford', which appears in the collection *Nocturnes* by John Connolly. The main protagonist, Adam Teal, is staying overnight at an inn when he encounters a ghostly presence in a bathroom that connects his room to another one.

Text 3A

Something warm and sticky touched Teal's bare feet, and he stepped back hurriedly to avoid the stream of viscous fluid that now poured slowly from the bathroom. The unseen presence struck the door, causing it to shudder, and then, as he watched, frozen despite himself, the knob slowly began to turn. Casting aside his lamp, Teal gripped the doorknob and pulled back with all his might. More clear liquid oozed from the bathroom keyhole, making his hands slippery. He felt a cry emerge from his lips, and began to shout.

'Help me,' he cried. 'Please help me. Someone is trying to enter my room!'

There was no reply. The presence on the other side of the door yanked hard at the handle, almost wrenching it from Teal's fingers. He gripped again, as tightly as he could, and lowered himself down slowly. Carefully, so as not to get any of the sticky paste on his face, he placed his right eye as close as he could to the keyhole.

At first he thought he could see nothing, except a vague whiteness, and he thought the substance had clogged the aperture entirely. Then the whiteness shifted, and Teal caught a glimpse of scorched flesh, damp with the sticky mucus, and grey-green legs, mottled with decay, and a distended stomach, swollen with gas. There was something about the shape of the body, the way that it moved.

(Connolly 2004: 482–3)

1   Comment on the way that the scene (characters and events) is construed in this extract.

2   What do you notice about degrees of specificity and how might you relate this to the genre of this short story?

3.3 Focus

Construing a scene also involves selecting and organizing that scene. In this section, we will focus on **scope**, which examines the coverage a particular word or phrase gives to some aspect of its conceptual content, and the notions of **profiling**, **windowing** and **figure-ground**, which provide a systematic way of explaining how our attention is focused on specific aspects of a scene so as to foreground some aspects and defocus or background others.

3.3.1 Scope

Our eyes can only ever afford us a limited viewing frame in so far as there are limits on what we can focus on at one time. This is a matter both of what is physically possible (our eyes face forwards so can only see what is in front of us rather than a 360 degree perspective) and what we naturally organize into some kind of ordered whole so that we are able to focus on some particular aspect ahead of another. This second aspect is an integral part of the notion of figure-ground that we will explore in Section 3.3.3.

As we saw in Chapter 2, lexical choices provide mental access to sets of cognitive domains that contain various kinds of knowledge that speakers/writers and listeners/readers hold. However, words and phrases also inherently

Figure 3.4 Maximal and immediate scope

provide some kind of boundary in so far as they mark off a particular portion of a cognitive domain so that a specific part of it is focused.

As an example, consider the word 'petal'. Although this particular word provides mental access to the concept of a flower (we know that a petal is part of a flower), it evokes one particular aspect of it. This conceptual relationship forms the basis for how and why we use particular words and how these words and their associated concepts work together in part-whole relationships. In cognitive grammar, this relationship is understood in terms of what is known as an expression's **maximal scope** (MS), the wider domain that an expression provides access to and its **immediate scope** (IS), the focused onstage portion of it. Thus, the word 'petal' has the maximal scope of the concept of a flower and an immediate scope of the top of the flower within which 'petal' is profiled as in the image of a tulip in Figure 3.4 (see also Section 3.3.2).

In texts, the maximal and immediate scopes evoked by an expression can yield interesting interpretative effects. For example, read Text 3B, an extract from Chapter 11 of Joseph Conrad's novel *The Secret Agent*. In this extract, Mrs Verloc is about to avenge the death of her brother, Stevie, by killing the man responsible, her husband, Mr Verloc.

Text 3B

She started forward at once, as if she was still a loyal woman bound to that man by an unbroken contract. Her right hand skimmed slightly the end of the table, and when she had passed on towards the sofa the carving knife had vanished without the slightest sound from the side of the dish. Mr

Verloc heard the creaky plank in the floor, and was content. He waited. Mrs Verloc was coming. As if the homeless soul of Stevie had flown for shelter straight to the breast of his sister, guardian and protector, the resemblance of her face with that of her brother grew at every step, even to the droop of the lower lip, even to the slight divergence of the eyes. But Mr Verloc did not see that. He was lying on his back and staring upwards. He saw partly on the ceiling a clenched hand holding a carving knife. It flickered up and down. Its movements were leisurely. They were leisurely enough for Mr Verloc to recognize the limb and the weapon.

(Conrad [1907] 2007: 197)

In this extract, it is interesting that Conrad emphasizes Mrs Verloc's hand as a clausal agent (see Chapter 5) in 'her right hand skimmed slightly the end of the table' and 'a clenched hand holding a carving knife' rather than using the expression 'Mrs Verloc' or 'his wife' or 'the woman'. The word 'hand' has the maximal scope of a body but an immediate scope of an arm and a possible interpretative effect is that the reader is asked to disconnect the body part from the whole person of Mrs Verloc in order to make her action appear involuntary and, arguably, more chilling since the hand is construed as working on its own. The restricted viewing frame evoked by the scope of the word 'hand' denies the reader direct access to the whole character of Mrs Verloc; this choice could be interpreted as downplaying her conscious role to the point that it foregrounds an unnatural and sinister kind of agency.

We can also see an interesting distinction in scope between non-progressive and progressive verb forms. For example,

- Anna drew a picture (non-progressive form)
- Anna was drawing a picture (progressive form)

In the first example, the verb's maximal and immediate scope are the same. The finite non-progressive verb form construes a maximal viewing frame that allows us to see the entire process (the drawing of the picture) from start to finish. In contrast, in the non-finite progressive form, the start and end-points of the process fall outside of the construal; effectively, although we know Anna must have started to draw, and that she will finish her drawing, the viewing frame we have on the event is restricted to some portion of that process in between the start and finish points. In other words, while the maximal scope of the process incorporates the entire event, the use of progressive form provides an immediate scope that only allows us to see a portion of the scene. In this way, the use of progressive forms creates an effect that is similar to peering in without experiencing the entire event. This can be seen in Figure 3.5. The grey box represents the part of the scene construed by a progressive form.

Figure 3.5 Maximal and immediate scope in –ing forms (adapted from Langacker 2008: 65)

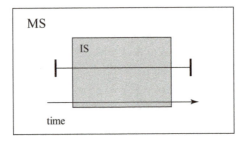

Activity 3.2: Progressive forms in poetry

One of the effects of using progressive verb forms is that events can be construed as being close by; it feels as though we have a more intimate and internal overview of a scene rather than a more global one. With this in mind, read Text 3C, an extract from 'The cataract of Lodore' by the nineteenth-century poet Robert Southey. The poem describes the Lodore Falls in Cumbria (a cataract is a large or high waterfall).

Text 3C

The cataract strong
Then plunges along,
Striking and raging

As if a war raging
Its caverns and rocks among;
Rising and leaping,
Sinking and creeping,
Swelling and sweeping,
Showering and springing,
Flying and flinging,
Writhing and ringing,
Eddying and whisking,
Spouting and frisking,
Turning and twisting,
Around and around
With endless rebound:
Smiting and fighting,
A sight to delight in;

Confounding, astounding,
Dizzying and deafening the ear with its sound.

(Southey [1820] 1876: 164)

What do you think is the effect of the use of verbs in this extract?

3.3.2 Profiling

As previously discussed, the expression 'petal' evokes the maximal scope of an entire flower and the immediate scope of the top of it. Within this immediate scope, 'petal' is profiled as the specific focus of attention against a **conceptual base** that acts as the background for understanding the profiled aspect.

The notion of profiling allows us to be more specific when examining the attention given to a particular aspect of a scene in relation to its conceptual base. For example, the words 'stamen', 'pistel' and 'sepal' have the same maximal and immediate scope as 'petal' but profile different parts of the conceptual base, namely, a specific part of the flower.

Many expressions and ways of talking about concepts rely on our ability to profile one portion of content in relation to a larger base. One example is the way we conceive and talk about time. For example, 'June' evokes the conceptual base of the Western calendar year and profiles the sixth month, 'Monday' evokes the conceptual base of a week and profiles the first day and '2:00 am' evokes the conceptual base of a day and profiles the second hour.

The notion of profiling can also be used to outline how metonymy, introduced in Chapter 2, operates. As we discussed in that chapter, expressions that are metonymic in nature include part-whole substitutions – for example, in a newspaper headline 'England need clear heads to keep the Ashes', where 'clear heads' refers to the players in the team, or when using the name of an artist to stand in for their work as in 'I've got to read Keats this semester'. In the second example, 'Keats' is used to evoke the poet's work within a broader domain of knowledge about him.

In both of these examples, an expression that would normally be used to profile one aspect of a particular domain is used to profile an alternative one within the same domain. For example, 'Keats' would normally simply profile the person, but the word can be used metonymically to profile different aspects associated with him and which are relative to the conceptual base of Keats as a famous writer.

Activity 3.3: Identifying scope and profile

Look at the list of words below.

1 Finger

2 Knuckle

3 Door

4 Keyhole

5 Door hinge

6 Steering wheel

7 London

8 Kent

1 Identify each word's maximal scope (MS) and immediate scope (IS).

2 Identify what is profiled (P) in each example.

3.3.3 Attentional windowing

Our discussion of scope and profiling demonstrates that language is inherently attention-seeking, in that any particular expression chosen by a user foregrounds that choice and its conceptual content and, by consequence, downplays other ones. We can also say that the focusing of our attention on 'petal' windows our attention: the analogy is of someone looking through a window where whatever is in the frame is the object of attention and whatever is outside of the frame is not available for viewing. Profiling 'petal' equally backgrounds or excludes other aspects such as 'stem' which remains outside of the viewing frame.

The concept of **windowing** offers a useful framework to use when examining the different possible construals of an event that exist along a path of motion. For example, imagine these four construals of a journey:

- They travelled from London via Guildford to Portsmouth
- They travelled from London
- They travelled to Portsmouth
- They travelled via Guildford

Each of these construals presents the same event but windows a different portion of it. In the first, the windowing of attention is on the whole journey but in the second the windowed aspect is the starting point, and in the third example it is the end point. Other portions of the journey in these examples are excluded or **gapped** from the construal. In the fourth example, the

Figure 3.6 Initial, medial and final windowing

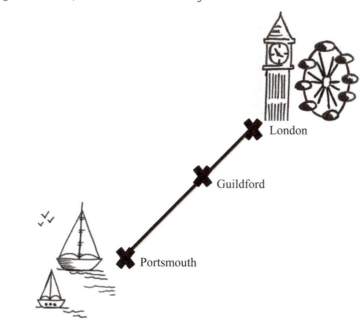

windowing of attention is on the middle part of the journey; the start and end points (London and Portsmouth, respectively) are omitted from the construal.

We can label these different windows according to the portions of the path that are afforded attention. Figure 3.6 shows the London to Portsmouth journey, and we can subsequently draw attention to a part of that journey through **full**, **initial**, **final** or **medial windowing**.

- They travelled from London via Guildford to Portsmouth (full windowing)
- They travelled from London (initial windowing)
- They travelled to Portsmouth (final windowing)
- They travelled via Guildford (medial windowing)

Interestingly, we can also window combinations of the initial, final and medial portions of a scene and to gap one aspect of the journey. So it would be possible to have construals such as:

- They travelled from London via Guildford (initial and medial windowing; final gapping)
- They travelled via Guildford to Portsmouth (medial and final windowing; initial gapping)
- They travelled from London to Portsmouth (initial and final windowing; medial gapping)

Activity 3.4: Attentional windowing in fiction

You can apply the concepts of windowing and gapping to literary texts by drawing on plot as a particular type of path and exploring those aspects that are windowed and gapped. Look at Text 3D, 'A Second Chance', a short story by Jay Bonestell.

Text 3D

His love had gone. In despair, he flung himself off the Golden Gate Bridge. Coincidentally, a few yards away a girl made her own suicide plunge.
The two passed in midair
Their eyes met.
Their chemistry clicked.
It was true love.
They realised it.
Three feet above the water.

(Bonestell 1995: 68)

1   How might you describe what is presented here in terms of windowing and gapping?
2   What might you say about the possible interpretative effects of these construals?

3.3.4 Figure and ground

The examples previously discussed demonstrate how we naturally foreground aspects of a scene through the expressions we use. For instance, 'petal' foregrounds the concept of a specific part against a larger conceptual backdrop of an entire flower; here the immediate scope is given focus against the background of the maximal scope. In a similar way, the use of progressive verb forms foregrounds a particular portion of an event so as to give a restricted viewing frame against a background of the entire event.

In cognitive grammar – and cognitive linguistics more generally – the way that we organize material in a scene in a particular way is understood as a manifestation of the phenomenon of **figure-ground**. For example, look at Figure 3.7. In this figure, what you see will either be a framed black cross (against a white background) or four white boxes against a black background. One part of the image will always stand out against the other, and although you can move (or toggle) between the two, it is impossible to see both at the same time.

Figure 3.7 demonstrates our natural tendency to configure what we see into a figure-ground relationship. In many cases, however, the relationship

Figure 3.7 Figure and ground

may be determined by the nature of objects or entities and their relationship within the scene itself. For instance, imagine looking out of a window and seeing a house in a field opposite. In this instance you would see a certain type of arrangement with some aspects of the scene afforded attention – for example, the house would typically be smaller, more defined and a different colour in relation to broader aspects such as the sky and the surrounding landscape which would remain in the background. The relationship in the scene is essentially a dynamic one, however, and could be reconfigured so that other entities are brought into perspective and previous ones become part of the background. For example, you could shift your attention to a tree that stands in the front garden of the house and reconfigure the house itself as the background. Both of these arrangements allow us to differentiate between the figure (the entity that stands out) and the ground (the de-emphasized background aspects). Generally speaking, figures tend to be smaller, brighter and have greater delineation and/or movement than the ground.

The principle of figure-ground also operates grammatically. For example, in English we would normally construe the first scene described as 'the house in the field' so that the grammar of the clause mirrors our conceptualization of the visually smaller entity, the house; it would generally feel less natural to give prominence in the clause to the ground in an expression like 'the field around the house'. Similarly, a new figure-ground relationship is enacted in the second scene so that a more natural construal would be in the expression 'the tree in front of the house', mirroring the spatial arrangement of the figure (tree) against the ground (house). Again, using 'the house behind the tree' does not quite sound right.

One of the most obvious examples of figure-ground in operation at clause level can be seen in the distinction between the active and passive voice:

- I broke the window (active voice: the agent 'I' is the clausal subject/figure against the ground of the object);
- The window was broken by me (passive voice: here the patient 'the window' is the clausal subject/figure and the agent is defocused as the ground).

The figure-ground distinction can also be scaled up from the level of the clause to account for the different ways in which we give prominence to aspects of a whole text at the expense of others. For example, we can examine the figure-ground relationship to look at how readers might be positioned to adopt a certain interpretation or preferred response to a text. A character that is consistently construed as a figure across a short story or novel might be considered more powerful or appealing. Equally, readers themselves may give prominence to certain ideas and responses when they talk or write about texts, at any one time placing some issue or response as a figure against the ground of others. This phenomenon can be seen in literary criticism. For example, responses (both academic and non-academic) to Shakespeare's *The Merchant of Venice* over the years have shifted between feeling sympathy towards the character of Shylock due to the way society treats him and viewing him as mean and cruel and deserving of his fate at the end of the play. Interpretative stances such as these automatically configure figure-ground status so that one interpretation is afforded prominence over another.

Activity 3.5: Figure-ground and design

We can see the principles of figure-ground configuration at work in texts that rely on some visual aspect. Text 3E is the front of a Christmas card. What do you notice about the way the designer has drawn on these principles?

Text 3E: The front of a Christmas card

3.4 Perspective

So far we have examined the phenomenon of construal in terms of what we select and focus our attention on in using different expressions. In this section, we turn to the overall viewing position we take from which we construe scenes and events.

As an example, let us return to our stage analogy again. Generally, the audience's position relative to the stage and the entities thereon affects what can be seen and consequently potential construals. Now, imagine the scene on the stage contains an actor and a table. How we construe that particular relationship depends on where in the audience we are sitting. For example, imagine viewing positions A and B.

In viewing position A (audience at the side of the stage), a natural construal would be 'the actor is next to the table' since the two entities appear side to side from the audience's perspective.

In viewing position B (audience at the front of the stage), a natural construal would be 'the actor is in front of the table' since the audience's line of sight extends through the actor to the table.

Figure 3.8 Viewing position A

Figure 3.9 Viewing position B

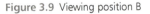

3.4.1 Vantage points

The discussion above is captured in the cognitive grammar notion of **vantage point**, which relates to the viewing position a conceptualizer assumes in the act of construal. In our discussion of the two situations, we could, of course, have included 'situation C' as a further **fictive vantage point** to imagine what the scene might look like were we to assume other viewing positions. An affordance of language is that it allows us to assume fictive positions such as 'If you were standing at the back of the stage, the table would be in front of the man', which takes into account the reconfigured line of sight of someone standing in and viewing from that particular position; the fictive nature of the vantage point is evident in the hypothetical if-clause within which the construal is framed.

Often, expressions inherently assume a particular vantage point. This is the case with a **deictic verb** such as 'come' and 'go', both of which denote kinds of movement either towards or away from the person speaking to them. For example, look at Figure 3.10.

In the first utterance, the speaker is at the top of a staircase and the hearer at the bottom. As motion is directed towards the speaker, the vantage point is shown using the verb 'come'. In the second example, however, the speaker is directing the hearer away from their location. In this instance, the verb 'go' is used to signal that the vantage point is one from which movement originates rather than arrives at. Both deictic verbs thus point outwards either towards (come) or from (go) what is known as the deictic centre, which acts as the point of origin of an utterance.

Figure 3.10 'Come' and 'go'

Now read Text 3F, an extract from 'City of Glass', part 1 of Paul Auster's *The New York Trilogy*. In this extract the protagonist, Quinn, has been employed to follow a man called Stillman. Quinn is waiting at a train station in the hope of seeing Stillman there.

Text 3F

Quinn watched them all, anchored to his spot, as if his whole being had been exiled to his eyes. Each time an elderly man approached, he braced himself for it to be Stillman. They came and went too quickly for him to indulge in disappointment, but in each old face he seemed to find an augur of what the real Stillman would be like.

(Auster 1985: 54–5)

In literature we are often asked to take on the vantage point of characters other than ourselves (something of course we cannot do in real life). In this extract, we assume the vantage point of Quinn, shifting our own perspective to that of his as he conceptualizes the events that are taking place in the fictional world. This vantage point is apparent in the use of the deictic verbs 'approached', 'came' and 'went', which all indicate aspects of movement either towards Quinn as in 'approached' and 'came' or, in the case of 'went', away from him. The specific construals are conceptualizer-centred in so far as they maintain a specific perspective on the fictional events as they unfold. In literature, such a vantage point is also known as point of view.

One interesting way that such construals can operate is to foreground certain ideological perspectives. For example, we saw in Section 3.3.3 that the way an event is construed in either the active or passive voice gives a certain prominence to the element that is positioned as the subject of the clause. Equally, political texts often demand that listeners and readers adopt a particular vantage point and deictic centre in relation to the conceptual content that is presented. For example, read Text 3G, a poster advertising from the Conservative Party to support their 2015 UK general election campaign.

Text 3G: Political poster from the 2010 general election

In this poster, the use of the imperative clause 'let's' containing the third-person plural pronoun (the contracted form of 'let us') conflates the positions of speaker and hearer into one so that they have a shared vantage point. The visual aspect of the poster with its straight road moving into the horizon depicts a viewpoint forwards-facing into the distance also serves to promote and foreground an ideological position from which the reader conceptualizes the future with the Conservative Party in government. The poster also makes use of metaphor, another specific type of construal. As we saw in Chapter 2, while metonymy construes one thing by referencing another entity in the same domain, metaphor construes one thing in terms of something else from a different domain. Usually, this involves something abstract (such as an emotion, experience or concept) being construed in terms of something concrete. Text 3.7 is underpinned both verbally and visually by the two conceptual metaphors LIFE IS A JOURNEY and PROGRESS IS AHEAD that construe the abstract notions of life and progress as movement along a path.

Of course, we can resist the way that such texts position us as readers. In fact, this poster was heavily criticized in media for both its message and the use of what were perceived as questionable claims and facts. Indeed it led to a number of parody posters that sought to undermine its central message and portrayal of the reality of a Conservative government.

3.4.2 Subjective and objective construal

The way in which a speaker or writer construes a scene can also be examined in relation to the extent to which the conceptualizer positions himself or

Figure 3.11 Objective and subjective construal (based on Verhagen 2007: 61–2)

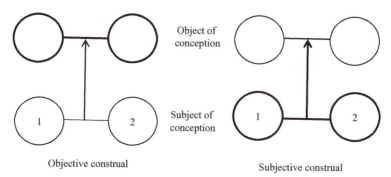

Objective construal   Subjective construal

herself in a particular viewing arrangement. Scenes may be construed objectively when they appear remote from a conceptualizer's own position, or subjectively when the conceptualizer is more involved to some degree. We will examine **subjective construal** and **objective construal** in more detail below.

Look at the following example,

- Zara ate the ice cream

In this example, the conceptualizers are the speaker/writer and listener/reader and the conceptualized content is the act of someone (Zara) eating an ice cream. We can also refer to the **subject(s) of conception** and the **object of conception** so as to draw attention to the respective roles relative to the act of conception (note that these terms are used in a different way to the standard definitions of the subject and object of a grammatical clause). In the process of conceptualization, one of the subjects (the speaker or writer) directs attention through the construal to the object so that it becomes part of the onstage region and in doing so aims to provide some sense of meaning that will be understood by the other subject (the listener or the reader).

In 'Zara ate the ice cream', we can say that the content is objectively construed since the subject of conception is not placed onstage and simply functions as a conceptualizing presence. Of course, the same content may be construed in a different way so as to foreground some aspect of the subject of conception. So in contrast, 'Zara may have eaten the ice cream' construes the content subjectively since now the conceptualizer's perspective on the scene is evident through the use of the modal auxiliary verb 'may' (see Chapter 6 for more on modality). We can see this difference in Figure 3.11, which shows the relative attention given to either the subject or object of conception in a particular construal.

In reality, absolute examples of objective and subjective construal are hard to find. Single words that simply identify either the object (e.g. 'tree') usually appear in longer structures such as phrases or clauses where some aspect of the ground is mentioned, and subjective utterances (e.g. 'hello') tend to figure where some part of the object of conception is also placed onstage (e.g. '"Hello!" the man said to his neighbour'). Consequently, it is much better to think about relative degrees of subjective and objective construal.

A further complexity occurs with the use of the pronouns 'I', 'you' and 'we'. Imagine the following construal of the same event.

- I'm sure that Zara ate the ice cream

In this instance, the conceptualized content is construed more subjectively but the subject of conception itself is also placed onstage, through the explicit use of the first-person pronoun 'I'. Here, the conceptualizer is also construed objectively as part of the overall scene. In contrast, our previous expression 'Zara may have eaten the ice cream' contains no additional construal of the self in such an objective way: the conceptualizer remains offstage. The same kind of blended perspective occurs if 'I' is replaced with 'we' or 'you' as follows.

- We watched the game: the use of 'we' places the conceptualizers (speaker/writer and listener/reader) onstage, which means that we construe them objectively. At the same time, the 'the game' becomes construed more subjectively, since we are more aware that the scene is being recounted through a particular perspective.
- You read the book: the use of 'you' places one of the conceptualizers (the listener/reader) onstage and objectively construed, while 'the book' presents a subjective construal offered by the other conceptualizer (the speaker/writer).

In some ways, then, we can think about levels of subjectivity/objectivity working in inverse tandem, depending on how prominent the speaker or conceptualizer is in relation to the scene being described. In other words, when the conceptualizer becomes more prominent and viewed more objectively, the scene that is being conceptualized becomes more subjective.

Figure 3.12 Continuum of construal

Figure 3.12 demonstrates how this relationship works. The image on the left shows an oasis, and, since our focus is entirely on the oasis itself, this image is objectively construed. In this instance we might imagine the construal to be something like 'There is an oasis in the desert'. The middle image, however, shows a cowboy looking at the scene. Here, the conceptualizer of the scene (the cowboy) is also placed onstage. While he becomes part of the object of the conceptualization, this means that the oasis is construed more subjectively than the first image since we now know it is being viewed, in part, through an additional perspective. In this instance we might imagine the construal as '"I can see an oasis in the desert" said the cowboy'. Finally, the presence of the thought bubbles in the final image on the right shows the most subjective construal of the scene, because here the conceptualizer is the most objectively construed. In this construal, which might be something like 'The cowboy dreamed of an oasis in the desert', we know that the scene is being filtered through the cowboy's daydream, and consequently he is positioned even more centrally onstage as the conceptualizer. As a result, the oasis becomes more subjectified, and arguably, more backgrounded relative to the cowboy's framing of the scene.

Activity 3.6: Subjective and objective construal

Read the following two texts. Text 3H is an extract from the beginning of *Worst Fears* by Faye Weldon. Text 3I is an extract from the beginning of *Embassytown* by China Mieville.

Text 3H

As Vilna and Abbie got into Abbie's little car, Diamond the Labrador jumped up at Vilna. Now there was mud all over Vilna's frilly white blouse. Vilna shoved the animal away with the side of her knee-high boot and then tried to get him in the crotch with a high heel. She missed. So Diamond ran round to the driver's side and leapt up at Abbie. Abbie was wearing an old grey sweater and didn't mind. Diamond wouldn't try Vilna again: he was accustomed to animal lovers. Vilna's rejection of him had made a great impression.

'Poor dog,' said Abbie. 'Poor dog. He's lost his master. He's bound to be upset.'

(Weldon 1997: 1)

Text 3I

When we were young in Embassytown, we played a game with coins and coin-sized crescent offcuts from a workshop. We always did so in the same place, by a particular house, beyond the rialto in a steep-sloping backstreet of tenements, where advertisements turned in colours under the ivy. We played in the smothered light of those old screens, by a wall we christened for the tokens we played with. I remember spinning a heavy two-sou piece on its edge and chanting as it went, *turnabout, incline, pig-snout, sunshine*, until it wobbled and fell. The face that showed and the word I'd reached when the motion stopped would combine to specify some reward or forfeit.

I see myself clearly in wet spring and in summer, with a deuce in my hand, arguing over interpretations with other girls and with boys. We would never have played elsewhere, though that house, about which and about the inhabitant of which there were stories, could make us uneasy.

Like all children we mapped our hometown carefully, urgently and idiosyncratically. In the market we were less interested in the stalls than in a high cubby left by lost bricks in a wall, which we always failed to reach. I disliked the enormous rock that marked the town's edge, which had been split and set again with mortar (for a purpose I did not know yet), and the library, the crenellations and armature of which felt unsafe to me. We all loved the college for the smooth plastone of its courtyard, on which tops and hovering toys travelled for metres.

(Mieville 2011: 7)

1   What do you notice about the ways in which scenes are construed?
2   Given that the conceptualizers are the writer/narrator and reader, what interpretative effects do you think that the particular construals have?

3.5 Extended example analysis

The following section draws together all the ideas and concepts covered in this chapter in an example analysis of Text 3J, an extract from Emma Donoghue's novel *Room*. The narrator, Jack, is a five-year-old boy who is being kept captive in a small 'Room' with his mother. Jack, however, is unaware that he is trapped or that the world exists beyond the confines of his captivity; he believes that the only real events and entities are those of the room that he is in. The following analysis draws on the notion of construal to examine the representation of Jack's mind style (Fowler 1977) in order to highlight the specific language choices that provide access to a character's view of the world. Such choices reveal insights about a character's ways of thinking, their cognitive abilities and the specific contexts that influence their conceptualizations of people, places and events.

Text 3J

We have thousands of things to do every morning, like give Plant a cup of water in Sink for no spilling, then put her back on her saucer on Dresser. Plant used to live on Table but God's face burned a leaf of her off. She has nine left, but they're the wide of my hand with furriness all over, like Ma says dogs are. But dogs are only TV. I don't like nine. I find tiny leaf coming, that counts as ten.

Spider's real. I've seen her two times. I look for her now but there's only a web between Table's leg and her flat. Table balances good, that's pretty tricky, when I go on one leg I can do it for ages but then I always fall over. I don't tell Ma about Spider. She brushes webs away, she says they're dirty but they look like extra-thin silver to me. Ma likes the animals that run around eating each other on the wildlife planet but not real ones. When I was four I was watching ants walking up Stove and she ran and splatted them all so they wouldn't eat our food. One minute they were alive and the next minute they were dirt. I cried so my eyes nearly melted off. Also another time there was a thing in the night *nnnnng nnnnng nnnnng* biting me and Ma banged him against Door Wall below shelf, he was a mosquito. The mark is still there on the cork even though she scrubbed, it was my blood the mosquito was stealing, like a teeny vampire. That's the only time my blood ever came out of me.

Ma takes her pill from the silver pack that has twenty-eight little spaceships and I take a vitamin from the bottle with the boy doing a handstand and she takes one from the big bottle with a picture of a woman doing Tennis. Vitamins are medicine for not getting sick and going back to Heaven yet. I never want to go, I don't like dying but ma says it might be OK when we're a hundred and tired of playing. Also she takes a killer. Sometimes she takes two, because things are good for us but suddenly too much is suddenly bad.

(Donoghue 2010: 10)

The construals in this extract are largely a result of Jack's experience of living in the 'Room' and his lack of knowledge of the outside world. In many ways, the extract is interesting to explore in terms of mind style as Jack's language contains both the restricted and ordinary world view of a child and a world view that deviates from convention due to the specific context Jack finds himself in. Throughout this extract, Jack's construals set up an opposition between what he is able to see and experience in the 'Room' and which he is told is real and his understanding of what isn't. His mother has told him that the entities, events and situations he sees on their television are fictional and Jack consequently uses 'TV' adjectivally to mean something like 'not real'.

One of the most striking features of Jack's language is that several count nouns are given the highest level of specificity through being construed as a proper noun, complete with a capital letter. These include 'Plant', 'Sink', 'Dresser' and 'Table'. A proper noun denotes the highest level of specificity since it identifies the referent as a single instance of a broader category (see also Chapter 6 for discussion of this). Thus, because Jack is unaware that other instances of plants, sinks, dressers and tables exist outside of the 'Room', he construes these more general categories as single, unique instances.

Throughout the extract there are also examples where Jack's construals of objects are much more schematic. For example, his description of the leaves, 'with furriness all over' and his reliance on 'the thing' and the non-lexical onomatopoeia of '*nnnnng nnnnng nnnnng*' when relaying the story of the mosquito are both evidence of his tendency (repeated at other points in the novel) to underlexicalize: he does not have the required vocabulary to be able to construe these entities more fully and so resorts to lexical items that he does possess. A further example of this is his use of the more general verb in 'doing Tennis' instead of the conventional 'playing Tennis'. He does, however, use the finely granular 'extra-thin silver' to describe the spider's webs, which demonstrates a greater complexity to his vocabulary, including the ability to produce creative construals based on analogy/metaphor (the domain of the precious metal 'silver' is used to access and richly define the spider's webs). This type of construal can also be seen in his description of the dead ants as 'dirt' and towards the end of the extract when Jack refers to the tablets his mother has as 'twenty-eight little spaceships' (the metaphor works due to the shape and colour of the tablets).

An additional metaphorical construal is 'God's face' that Jack uses when talking about the sun. We are told a couple of pages earlier that there is a small skylight in the room that Jack and his mother are kept in, and Jack's construal here is again the consequence of his context and limited knowledge of the world. Indeed, since his mother has told him that there is no reality outside of the 'Room', Jack is only able to understand the sun's rays in such terms. The construal thus works by framing something that Jack cannot understand and see clearly in terms of something much more immediate and concrete (a face) even if his mother has told him that it belongs to 'God'.

It is also interesting to observe how Jack both construes events that have taken place and relays those events to the reader. He often uses a progressive verb form, 'I find tiny leaf coming', 'eating each other', 'I was watching ants', 'there was a thing . . . biting me', which makes the events feel immediate and temporally close; these processes are scanned in a summary rather than a sequential fashion (see Chapter 4 for more on scanning).

Finally, clearly much of this extract contains subjective construal since Jack places himself onstage as an object of conception and is construed objectively by the reader in addition to the subjective construal of the content he himself narrates. The continued focus on the self gives rise to an intense feel to the extract during which the reader is given intimate access to Jack's way of seeing the world. The reader is also acutely aware, even if Jack is not, of how context (the physical location and the fact that his mother hides the truth about their existence from him) constrains the construal options available to him.

3.6 Further activities

1.

Read Text 3K, 'Anthem for Doomed Youth' by Wilfred Owen who was a soldier and a poet during the First World War. The poem reflects on the experiences and deaths of soldiers and the ways in which they will be remembered in time.

Text 3K

What passing-bells for these who die as cattle?
   – Only the monstrous anger of the guns.
   Only the stuttering rifles' rapid rattle
Can patter out their hasty orisons.
No mockeries now for them; no prayers nor bells;
   Nor any voice of mourning save the choirs, –
The shrill, demented choirs of wailing shells;
   And bugles calling for them from sad shires.

What candles may be held to speed them all?
   Not in the hands of boys, but in their eyes
Shall shine the holy glimmers of goodbyes.
   The pallor of girls' brows shall be their pall;
Their flowers the tenderness of patient minds,
And each slow dusk a drawing-down of blinds.

(Owen [1920] 1994: 1994: 12)

1 What interests you about the poem in respect of how the soldiers and other aspects of the battlefield are construed in the first stanza?

2 What do you notice about the perspective that the speaking voice takes in the second stanza? Can you explain it in terms of the cognitive grammar notion of vantage point?

2.

Read Text 3L, an extract from *Breathless: An American Girl in Paris*, an auto-biographical account by the American writer Nancy K. Miller of her time spent in Paris as a young woman in the 1960s. In this section, she writes about persuading her friend Valerie to drive her to Venice to meet up with Leo, a young man she has been seeing in Paris.

Text 3L

We left the Fiat in an open lot near the Piazzale di Roma and walked to the youth hostel where we planned to meet Leo for our first night in Venice. It was late and we decided to leave our suitcases in the car since we'd be moving to a hotel early the following day. By the next morning, when Valerie and I returned to pick up our luggage, the car had been picked clean. We stared at the empty car for a few minutes without speaking, stunned by our bad luck.

After two hours of declarations to the police, shrugged shoulders conveyed the official response of the plight of American girls leaving their belongings in a car with telltale TT license plates on Christmas Eve. 'Peccato, signorine.' That's a pity. Anyway, it was 'la Festa', and everything was shut down for the holidays. Valerie glared at me as if I were entirely to blame, and maybe I was, given my true motive for luring her to Italy. I was less willing to take the blame in the required filial letter: 'I'm worried that you'll think I'm irresponsible, etc. but is it really my fault?' I hated losing things, but I also hated knowing that by return mail my own feeling of loss would be drowned in the vast ocean of parental ire.

(Miller 2013: 25–6)

What do you notice about the way that events in this extract are construed in terms of specificity, vantage points and subjective/objective construal?

3.

Find a text that you think is interesting in terms of how events are construed. Explain what effects the various construals have on you as a reader using your learning from this chapter. Now experiment by rewriting parts of the texts drawing on alternative construals based on specificity, focus and prominence and perspective. What effects do your rewriting have? You could re-examine the choices made by the writer of the original text in light of your own interventions.

3.7 Further reading

Chapter 3 of Langacker (2008) provides a broad overview of construal in cognitive grammar. There is also coverage in Chapter 1 of Taylor (2002), in Chapter 2 of Radden and Dirven (2007) and throughout Ungerer and Schmid (2006). Verhagen (2007) and Harrison et al. (2014) also offer a very accessible and useful account of the phenomenon. Verspoor (1996) explores the notion of scope by discussing 'ing' forms and how they construe events as being close by. Talmy (2000a) outlines the operational aspects of windowing and there is a short but very useful section on the attentional system in Evans and Green (2006). Good coverage of figure-ground can be found in Talmy (2000a), Ungerer and Schmid (2006) and Stockwell (2019). Stockwell (2009) maps out his attention-resonance model and an inventory of the features of good textual attractors that can be used to examine the dynamic nature of figure-ground configurations in discourse. Stockwell (2019) also explores cognitive deixis. Viewing arrangements and subjective/objective construal are examined in Langacker (1991). Work in stylistics that addresses concepts covered in this chapter is exemplified across a number of chapters in Harrison (2017a). The effects of profiling are examined in Neary (2014) (on poetry) and in Pleyer and Schneider (2014) (on multimodal texts). The effects of Conrad's construals in the extract from *The Secret Agent* (Text 3.2) are explored, from a systemic-functional linguistic perspective, in Kennedy (1982) and also in Simpson (2014a). Giovanelli (2018b) uses cognitive grammar to analyse a similar construal in the opening of Neil Gaiman's *The Graveyard Book*. Giovanelli (2014a) examines the interpretative and conceptual effects of progressive verb forms in Sassoon's 'A Working Party', and Harrison (2014) utilizes attentional windowing to examine postmodernist fiction. Equally, Esmaeili and Asadi Amjad (2016) explore the textual properties of attentional windowing as well as considering how an analysis can be enriched by drawing conceptual metaphor, schema and force dynamics. Harrison (2017b) and Giovanelli (2018a) cover construal generally including a discussion of subjective and objective construal and the representation of a character's mind style. Nuttall (2015) utilizes the notion of construal to explore mind style and reader empathy in Richard Matheson's novel *I am Legend*. Nuttall (2018) examines construal in a book-length treatment of speculative fiction. Hart (2013, 2014a,b, 2015, 2016) provides work on applying the notion of construal to non-literary texts, integrating it into Critical Discourse Analysis (CDA) to examine political and multimodal discourse.

Chapter 4
Nouns and verbs

Key objectives

In this chapter we will explore:

- the semantic classification of nouns and verbs within cognitive grammar;
- the relationship between noun and verb schemas, and how these connections work up to the level of a clause;
- how we conceptually scan events in language; and
- how these ideas might account for patterns in clauses and longer stretches of text.

4.1 Noun and verb schemas

Nouns and verbs are the nuts and bolts of language. Most of us are familiar with the general distinction that verbs are 'doing' words, whereas nouns are 'things'. Following this basic contrast, most grammarians agree that nouns and verbs are seen as conceptual opposites, with verbs conceptually dependent on a noun that performs the action:

Table 4.1 Archetypes for nouns and verbs, after Langacker (2008: 104)

	Archetype for Nouns	Archetype for Verbs
Composition	Material substance	Energy transfer
Time	Indefinite location	Bound in time
Space	Bound in space	Dependent on location of participant(s)
Conceptualization	Conceptually autonomous	Conceptually dependent

The archetypes listed in Table 4.1 support the prototypical view that, generally speaking, nouns are objects and verbs are actions.

In cognitive grammar, however, nouns and verbs are treated more schematically. Although it is useful to broadly differentiate between nouns and verbs as in Table 4.1, in cognitive grammar it is argued that grammatical class is not an inherent part of a word, but rather that this classification is dependent upon the speaker/writer's construal of the word. This is one of cognitive grammar's most controversial claims, and one which proposes a dynamic and context-sensitive way of defining grammatical class. This claim emphasizes the semantic rather than the grammatical classification of words, and it also allows clear connections to be drawn between how nouns and verbs work differently in context.

Consider, for example, a word like 'fight', which can be used as a noun or a verb as the following three literary contexts demonstrate.

Text 4A

It was important, Dumbledore said, to fight, and fight again, and keep fighting, for only then could evil be kept at bay, though never quite eradicated.

(Rowling 2005: 644)

Half a dozen brats turned with expressions of derision, and Lyra threw her cigarette down, recognizing the cue for a fight.

(Pullman 1995: 55)

I don't petition to join the fighters, not that they would let me. I have no stomach for it anyway, no heat in my blood.

(Collins 2010: 211)

In the first sentence in Text 4A, the conceptualizer uses the word 'fight' as a verb, in both its infinitive ('to fight') and in its continuous forms ('keep fighting'). This sentence designates a relationship between a trajector (who is offstage here in that they are not explicitly mentioned, but is likely to be identified as Harry/Dumbledore, or perhaps 'good' as the antonym of the explicitly identified 'evil') who performs the action and the thing being fought against, the landmark ('evil').

In the second sentence, conversely, the narrator construes 'fight' as a noun, as indicated by the indefinite determiner 'a'. Here, the sentence gives prominence to the holistic event itself, in its **nominal** form. The first-person conceptualizer of the third sentence similarly construes 'fight' as a noun, but designates greater prominence to the agents ('the fighters') that perform the action.

The classification of grammatical class in these three sentences is a matter of profiling. As noted in Chapter 3, profiling occurs where attention is drawn to a particular section of a conceptual base (in the context of these three sentences, the word 'fight'). It was observed that a profile in language is the part of the sentence that holds our attention, whereas the base is the conceptual content that underlies the phrase. The conceptual base of the word 'fight' is, inherently, a process. In other words, whether used as a noun or as a verb, the concept 'fight' evokes a trajector who uses force against a landmark. This is the case for whether we construe the verb in its physical sense (as in the latter two sentences), or as part of a mental process, as suggested by its use in the first sentence.

Simply put, our mental conceptualization of a word like 'fight' comprises its potential to refer to an event, as a noun, and to be used as a process – one which can either be figurative or material. In all the contexts outlined in Text 4A, this conceptualization forms the conceptual base for our understanding of the word. In specific linguistic contexts, however, we can choose to profile it as a verb or as a noun.

Activity 4.1: Profiling in poetry

Consider Text 4B, the opening lines from beginning of Shakespeare's famous Sonnet 116.

Text 4B

Let me not to the marriage of true minds
Admit impediments. *Love* is not *love*
Which *alters* when it *alteration* finds,
Or bends with the *remover* to *remove*.

1 Identify the profiles for each word in italics. Is a noun or a verb being profiled? What is the conceptual base of each word?
2 Comment on the stylistic effects of these profiles in context. You might want to think about how your answers connect with cognitive grammar's treatment of encyclopaedic/schematic structures as introduced in Chapter 2.

4.2 Nouns and noun phrases

Once we have identified that a noun profile has been established, there are many further ways of classifying nominals within the cognitive grammar system.

4.2.1 Instances, types and determiners

In cognitive grammar, nouns can be further differentiated between a **type** and an **instance**. In isolation, the word 'book', for example, represents a type (i.e. a more general category), whereas the noun phrase 'the book' profiles one of many instances (i.e. a more specific example within the general category) (for more on this, see Chapter 6, Section 6.1.2).

'The' is often used to identify a particular instance in language. It is a **definite determiner** as it suggests a level of shared understanding between the speaker and the listener (or the writer and the reader), and indicates something that can be identified easily. Put simply, when we use 'the' we are pointing to something that we assume our addressee knows or will be able to recognize. Alternately, the determiner 'a' is an **indefinite determiner**. Though indefinite determiners also single out an instance for our attention, they are used in those situations where the object or entity is not as highly specified, or perhaps not as recognizable. Consider, for example, the difference between '*the* old red book' and '*an* old red book'.

An example of the relationship between instances and types, and the role determiners play in singling out instances can be seen in Text 4C, a section from the opening of the contemporary dystopian bestseller *The Maze Runner* (Dashner 2011). This novel opens in medias res. The protagonist, Thomas, arrives in an unknown location with severe memory loss. It transpires that this other place is called 'the Glade', and is populated with other boys of the same age as Thomas. Like the reader, Thomas has to piece together and make sense of this new surrounding world and the terms the other boys use to describe it.

Text 4C

Newt clapped him on the shoulder. 'Greenie, what you're feelin', we've all felt it. We've all had First Day, come out of that dark box. Things are bad, they are, and they'll get much worse for ya soon, that's the truth. But down the road a piece, you'll be fightin' true and good. I can tell you're not a bloody sissy.'

'Is this a prison?' Thomas asked; he dug in the darkness of his thoughts, trying to find a crack to his past.

'Done asked four questions, haven't ya?' Newt replied. 'No good answers for ya, not yet, anyway. Best be quiet now, accept the change – morn comes tomorrow.'

Thomas said nothing, his head sunk, his eyes staring at the cracked, rocky ground. A line of small-leafed weeds ran along the edge of one of the stone blocks, tiny yellow flowers peeping through as if searching for the sun, long disappeared behind the enormous walls of the Glade.

(Dashner 2011: 5)

Despite his memory loss, Thomas recognizes the types of things that underlie particular noun phrases mentioned in the conversation. This helps him – and us – to understand what is being referred to, without these ideas being explicitly introduced and defined. In the text, these noun phrases then become explicitly marked out as specific instances.

In the above exchange between Newt and Thomas, for example, 'First Day' is established as a specific event: an instance that, seemingly, the other boys have also experienced. Other noun phrases in the opening to the novel – references to the Glade (and its inhabitants, the Gladers), The Cliff, The Maze – are similarly marked as specific instances with a more general type through the use of definite determiners and capitalization (seen, in this extract, in the reference to 'the Glade').

These noun phrases are used to refer to distinct places and people within the context of this new world. The fact that these particular instances can be understood in relation to their wider types and associations, however, does lead to some continued disorientation on Thomas' part. Significantly, for example, he asks whether this new place is 'a prison' (possibly due to the reference to 'that dark box' and 'the enormous walls' that, in other contexts, schematically support this interpretation).

4.2.2 Mass nouns, count nouns and quantifiers

The particular parts of the scene that Thomas marks out within his surrounding environment in Text 4C are all **count nouns**: objects that can be counted and grouped. Typically, in cognitive grammar, count nouns are used to describe physical objects (and also other entities, such as ideas and places), whereas **mass nouns** refer to physical substances.

The distinction between these two types of nouns can be difficult to pin down in schematic terms, as these labels are used to describe prototypical groupings and do not necessarily represent categorical classifications of things. There is much debate about the relationship between the two types. As always, however, it is easiest to think about how the noun functions in context.

As the label suggests, count nouns describe things that can be counted and therefore can take the plural form when more than one instance of the same type is listed (as can be identified in Thomas' description in Text 4C: 'weeds', 'blocks', 'questions', 'flowers'), whereas mass nouns cannot (e.g. water, paper, wood). In addition to the presence or absence of the plural morpheme 's' as in these latter examples, the plural/singularity of count nouns can also be indicated using **quantifiers**. Quantifiers can either be proportional (e.g. some, most) or indicate a representative instance (e.g. any, each).

- *Some* books are worth reading. (proportional)
- *Each* book is worth reading. (representative instance)

Furthermore, count nouns can be used with an indefinite article, whereas mass nouns cannot. Instead, mass nouns can stand alone as a nominal expression (e.g. the more typical sentence would be an example like 'a book is made out of paper', rather than 'book is made out of a paper').

Like the explanation of nouns and verbs earlier in this chapter, the difference between these two types of quantifiers, and these two types of nouns, can be useful to consider in stylistics because it indicates the relationship between the thing being described against its more general type. It helps to explain how attention can be directed more specifically (as in Text 4C, where Thomas is clearly focusing on each new part of the surrounding scene) or more diffusely.

This contrast between the specific and the more general is also paralleled in verb schemas, as the next sections observe.

4.3 Verbs and verb phrases

4.3.1 Perfective and imperfective

One of the ways in which cognitive grammar subdivides verb schemas is to consider whether the process in question is **perfective**[1] or **imperfective**. To differentiate between these two types more generally, it can be said that a perfective verb refers to an event, whereas an imperfective verb refers to a state.

Perfective verbs are those that are bounded in time. In other words, these are verbs that profile a particular occurrence of an event, and ones that indicate a change through time. Consider, for example, a sentence like 'I *throw* the ball'. The verb 'throw' here is perfective; it describes a specific event that occurs at a particular moment. Imperfective verbs, on the other hand,

Figure 4.1 Imperfective (left) and perfective (right) verbs

Time   Time

are those that are not specifically bounded in time, and instead profile a stable situation that continues. A sentence like 'I *have* the ball', for example, is stative: the imperfective verb 'have' here describes an ongoing situation. The contrast in these two verb types can be represented as in Figure 4.1.

As we are beginning to observe in this chapter, like other grammatical categories the cognitive grammar distinction between these two types is context-dependent.

4.3.2 Scanning

Scanning refers to how language users track events through time. Cognitive grammar identifies two modes of scanning through which we process these state-relationships: **sequence scanning** and **summary scanning.**

In order to distinguish between the two types, a viewing metaphor is commonly used. We can compare sequence scanning to how we view a moving film, and summary scanning to how we view a multi-exposure photograph. The former refers to how we conceptualize an event changing seamlessly between states, whereas the latter refers to how particular states can be singled out for attention; and how the multiple states of an event can be imagined simultaneously. Figure 4.2, for example, shows a cat's descent from a tree. Each 'state' of the cat's trajectory is summatively singled out for our attention.

As another example, imagine you are watching someone swim a length in a swimming pool. Just one part of the swim – one state – is processed at any given moment. In other words, you can see the swimmer raise their arms and dive through the water, and can follow how they move from one

Figure 4.2 Summary scanning

end of the pool to the other in real time, or what is known as processing time. In cognitive grammar terms, this is known as a sequence scan: the process by which we keep track of an event, at each successive stage, as it is happening.

Of course, as you watch, your working memory helps you to remember the path previously taken by the swimmer – and you can also re-conceptualize a movement from a previous part of their swim, from an earlier moment. You might remember and visualize, for example, when the swimmer jumped into the pool at the start of their swim, or another point of their trajectory through the water. In cognitive grammar, this process would be classed as a summary scan. In this example, you are conceptualizing a state within the event that occurs out of time with the real-time viewing experience and also isolating one part of the event summatively, as in each stage of the cat's jump from the tree in Figure 4.2.

Activity 4.2: Scanning newspaper headlines

Read the headlines in Text 4D.

Text 4D

a Trump *swings* the majority

b May *leads* UK congratulations for the new president elect

c Trump's conversation with Farage *leaves* Britain leaders red-faced

d Trump *is* victorious

e Inside the mind of Theresa May

1 First, identify whether the verbs (in italics) in each headline are perfective or imperfective.

2 Second, consider how this distinction impacts upon how we scan each headline. What is the effect of representing the events in this way?

3 The final headline does not have a verb. How do we scan this headline?

4.4 Locating nouns in context

Imagine that you are walking down the road where you live and a passer-by asks for directions to the nearest post office. In order to explain where the post office is, you are likely to describe easily identifiable parts of the surroundings in order to help the person find it more easily. You might mention, for example, that it is opposite a large green park or that it is next to a supermarket.

In this scenario, you are drawing on **reference points** to locate something (in this example, the post office) alongside something else that is perhaps more distinctive (the large green park, or the supermarket). Reference points are useful because they can be used by speakers/writers to guide the listener's/reader's attention towards a particular part of the scene.

In this example, the post office is a **target**. Targets are things or parts of the scene that are less obvious or salient, but more easily identifiable when scanned alongside the initial reference point. The speaker in the following sentence, for instance, is attempting to describe a new book to the addressee by drawing a connection to another book that had previously been discussed:

- Do you remember that book (RP) we talked about last week? This book (T) is similar, but has a better plot.

Every expression has many potential targets (i.e. as a group, these targets are called the **dominion** of that reference point). The second example below, for instance, comprises multiple targets.

- Do you see that big blue vase (RP)? On the shelf below (T), next to the plant (T) is the book I mentioned on Wednesday (T).

Here, the speaker guides the listener's attention to the book 'mentioned on Wednesday' and does so by creating a reference point chain, drawing on successive targets ('the shelf below', 'the plant') in order to single out the final target, 'the book', in question. This is a useful strategy as it allows the speaker to locate a particular object by initially singling out the most salient reference point in the surrounding scene. As with the role of the park or the supermarket in the previous post office example, we assume that the 'big blue vase' is more visually prominent than the book itself, and therefore this mental path needs to be drawn in order for the listener to successfully locate it.

This process occurs in both real and fictional contexts. Texts written for young children, for example, often draw upon or emphasize reference point relationships. This is most obvious in children's books that pair images and text. In the book series *Funnybones*, for instance, parallel linguistic constructions help to guide children's attention from the initial reference point ('a dark, dark town') through a series of successive targets.

Activity 4.3: Reference points in children's fiction

Consider Text 4E, pages from the children's book *Funnybones: The Pet Shop*.

Text 4E

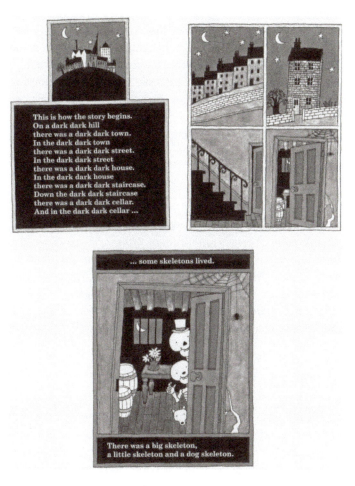

1 How do the images correspond with the reference points mentioned in the text?

2 How are the reference chains structured?

4.5 Other reference point relationships

In their original application, reference point relationships are used to describe general conceptual organization: such as that needed to construe relationships of nominal compounds, possession and metonymy.

4.5.1 Nominal compounds

A nominal compound is a noun phrase that comprises more than one noun, such as 'book worm'. In an expression like this, and in nominal compounds more generally, the first noun establishes the context for the second.

In the above example, for instance, 'book' works as a reference point to contextualize the meaning of the entire phrase. Within this context, we know that 'worm' should be construed as a person who loves reading, rather than the creature we would find in the garden. In other nominal compounds, reference points will signpost other contexts, and other instances: for example, 'earth worm', 'ear worm' and so on.

4.5.2 Possession

In possessives, reference points work in a similar way as they do in nominal compounds. Typically, the possessor acts as the reference point, and the entity possessed is the target. In the example, 'Rob's tea', for instance, it is clear that Rob is the initial reference point and focus of attention, and the 'tea' is the target; the item we contextualize in relation to Rob.

4.5.3 Metonymy

Reference points play an important role in understanding relationships of metonymy. In metonymy, a specific profile of a concept is used instead of naming the actual concept. For example, when we talk about 'the White House', people typically understand this phrase to refer to the president and other politicians, rather than to the physical building itself.

In examples of metonymy, the actual thing being described (in this last example, the president and his staff) – the target of the sentence – is offstage (i.e. not explicitly mentioned in the sentence).

Activity 4.4: Reference points in metonymy

Based on what you already know about reference points, how do you think reference point relationships work in metonymic expressions?

Consider, for example, the idiom: 'The pen is mightier than the sword'. What do we understand this expression to refer to? How is this expression manipulated in Text 4F, a cartoon by Rob Tornoe published in 2015 after the Charlie Hebdo attacks in France?

Text 4F

Reference points clearly play a key role in language, helping us to direct attention in order to highlight a particular person, thing or location. However, although some reference point relationships can be clearly and definitively marked (as in the three types of reference relationships mentioned here), reference points can also work at a broader level in language. Because references and targets relate to conceptual organization more generally, we cannot be too definitive about what constitutes as a reference point and what does not. In other words, the kinds of reference point relationships outlined here is not an exhaustive list of how they can be used in language.

Activity 4.5: Reference point chains in the opening of *Gone Girl*

Text 4G is from the opening page of Gillian Flynn's contemporary thriller *Gone Girl*. The novel starts with the day of Amy Dunne's disappearance, narrated through the perspective of her husband, Nick Dunne.

After you have read the passage, consider the questions below.

Text 4G

NICK DUNNE

THE DAY OF

When I think of **my wife**, I always think of **her head**. The shape of it, to begin with. The very first time I saw her, it was **the back of the head** I saw, and there was something lovely about it, **the angles of it**. Like a shiny, hard <u>corn kernel</u> or a <u>riverbed fossil</u>. She has what the Victorians would call a finely shaped head. You could imagine the skull quite easily.

I'd know **her head** anywhere.

And what's inside it. I think of that, too: **her mind**. **Her brain**, all those coils, and **her thoughts** shuttling through those coils like fast, frantic centipedes. Like a child, I picture opening **her skull**, unspooling **her brain** and sifting through it, trying to catch and pin down **her thoughts**. *What are you thinking, Amy?* The question I've asked most often during **our marriage**, if not out loud, if not to the person who could answer. I suppose these questions <u>stormcloud</u> over every marriage: *What are you thinking? How are you feeling? Who are you? What have we done to each other? What will we do?*

(Flynn 2012: 1, italics as in original)

1   What reference point chains can you identify in this passage?

2   The nominal compounds are underlined for you and the possessive relationships are highlighted in bold. What is the stylistic effect of Nick describing Amy in this way?

3   How is the point of view of the character Nick represented, in particular, through these stylistic choices? You might want to further consider the metaphorical language and verb profiles in your response.

4.6 Profiling 'Words': Extended example analysis

In order to draw together the ideas presented in this chapter, this next section presents an extended analysis of Text 4H, Sylvia Plath's poem 'Words'. The poem appears in Plath's collection *Ariel* that was first published in 1963.

Text 4H

Words

Axes
After whose stroke the wood rings,
And the echoes!
Echoes travelling
5   Off from the centre like horses.

The sap
Wells like tears, like the

Water striving
To re-establish its mirror
10 Over the rock

That drops and turns,
A white skull,
Eaten by weedy greens.
Years later I
15 Encounter them on the road –

Words dry and riderless,
The indefatigable, hoof-taps.
While
From the bottom of the pool, fixed stars
20 Govern a life.

(Plath 1963)

In 'Words', words are initially presented as axes: sharp or blunt, heavy and cutting. The poem is a statement on the art of writing; on the import and emotional impact of all words. Consequently, the lexical choices all carry a metaphorical meaning, which can be traced to four superordinate conceptual metaphors (see Chapter 2) that run throughout the poem:

- WORDS ARE AXES

- WORDS ARE HORSES

- EMOTIONS ARE WATER

- LIFE IS A JOURNEY

The first conceptual metaphor – WORDS ARE AXES – is apparent through juxtaposition of the first two noun profiles in the poem, the 'Words' of the title and the 'Axes' of the first line, but this metaphor is also reinforced later through semantic parallelism and the conceptual domains of other lexical choices: we might think of the flinty 'rock' (line 10), the hard but brittle 'mirror' (line 9), the bone of the 'skull' (line 12), the blade of the 'axe' (line 1). That 'stroke' describes the axe's action, however, invites two conceptualizations. In this context, 'stroke' becomes a contronym: a word that has contradictory definitions. A 'stroke' can be conceptualized as a gentle action, but when construed alongside the axe as an agent and point of reference, the opposite is conceptualized. This semantic ambivalence is reinforced throughout the poem.

The theme of movement and fluidity is paralleled in EMOTIONS ARE WATER, which in turn is evoked through the mass nouns 'sap' (line 6) and 'water' (line 8), and the count nouns 'tears' (line 7) and 'water' (line 8). The other metaphors are highlighted similarly through the choice of lexical items and semantic fields. A conceptualization of WORDS ARE HORSES, for example, is invited through the simile construction in line 5 ('like horses'), and later through the references to being 'riderless' (line 16) and the sound of 'indefatigable hoof-taps' (line 17), whereas LIFE IS A JOURNEY in turn is evoked through references to 'travelling', exemplified further through the verbs ('rings', 'encounter', 'striving'), the 'road', and a sense of chronological time as described in the noun phrase 'years later', and the time adverbial 'while'.

An image of ripples in water is also likely to be conceptualized by readers, despite not being nominalized directly at any point in the poem. Instead, the conceptual bases of the lexical choices, such as the shape of the 'wood rings' (line 2), the impression of reverberation created through 'Echoes travelling/ Off from the centre' (lines 4–5) and the attempt to restore a 'mirror' on the water's surface, all help to create a ripples motif. It is interesting to note that the 'mirror' of balance and equilibrium is paralleled in the punctuation: ten of the lines are end stopped, and the other ten display enjambment. This displays strong 'symbolic correspondence' (Croft 2001: 18) in the poem; or, in other words, a close, interdependent relationship between the poem's form and its meaning.

The organization of language in the poem creates semantic ambivalence in particular places. This can be seen, for example, in line 2, in the construction 'the wood rings'. Because of the syntax, 'rings' becomes a grammatical homonym. In other words, the construction is simultaneously profiled as a noun-noun compound (the 'wood rings' of a tree-trunk) and as a noun-verb construction (the wood 'rings' with the sound of the axe). In these alternate profiles, 'wood' works either as an agent (in the verb profile) or as a reference point (in the noun profile). The former construal is supported by reading the morpheme 's' as a marker of plurality (for count nouns) but, of course, this morpheme similarly functions to signpost a perfective verb. The construal of the verb profile of 'wood rings' is paralleled through the shared connotations of repetition and continuity that are features of the other sounds referenced in the poem: 'echoes' and 'hoof-taps'.

In a similar way to the 'wood rings' construction in line 2, the first two lines of the second stanza invite the reader to conceptualize alternate noun/verb profiles simultaneously:

The sap
Wells like tears

(Plath 1963)

Again, 'wells' here can be profiled as both a perfective verb, and, simultaneously, a count noun, marked grammatically as a plural. Like with the example of 'wood rings' in the first stanza, this example similarly invites the reader to imagine two construals, both of which are supported by the co-text. This level of self-reflexivity indicates a meta-awareness of how words work in context – entirely appropriate for a poem that forms a meditation on the art of writing.

Although the adjective-noun construction 'weedy greens' (line 13) in the third stanza does not invite simultaneous construals like the previous examples of simultaneous noun/verb profiles, it is inverted from the usual configuration: 'green weeds' would be a more typical collocation. In this construction 'weedy' becomes an evaluative adjective, rather than the potentially only descriptive and tautological 'green'. The 'greens' then become nominalized, a conversion that profiles and foregrounds the conceptualizations associated with this colour, such as jealousy and naivety. Similarly, the description of the 'skull' as 'white' is also semantically dissonant; are not skulls usually white? The appearance of the skull, when taken as a possible target for the reference point 'words' of the title, evokes the line of the familiar British school rhyme: 'sticks and stones may break my bones'. Rather than being 'broken', however, the skull is described as 'eaten' – a deviance that again suggests more menacing undertones.

Towards the end of the poem it is described how, 'years later' (line 14), the 'words dry' (line 16). 'Dry' is in the predicative position, a syntactic deviance making the phrase seem like a noun-verb string expressing fact-permanency: *ink* dries, and words consequently become 'indefatigable':

Words dry and riderless,
The indefatigable, hoof-taps.

(Plath 1963)

It could be construed that the caesura after 'indefatigable', coupled with the definite determiner 'the', nominalizes 'the indefatigable' as a noun phrase. This effect ironizes this particular construction: the word means 'unstoppable', or, 'untiring', and yet its profile as a noun renders the poem, and the 'words', static – they are 'dry' and therefore 'permanent'.

Other definite determiners in the poem identify specific noun profiles ('the echoes', 'the sap', 'the water', 'the rock', 'the road', etc.) but at the same time there are a number of unspecified noun profiles ('axes', 'echoes', 'horses', 'tears', 'mirror', etc.), and only two indefinite instances ('a white skull', 'a life'). This movement between the specified and the unspecified makes the poem seem both generalizable (these are concepts, places, ideas that represent general 'types' of situations), but, at the same time, distinctive and personal. Until stanza three, the narrator of these thoughts has been unmentioned. However, the deviant appearance of the first-person pronoun in the verb phrase 'I/Encounter' (lines 14–15) further personalizes the viewpoint of the poem. The coupling of this pronoun with the objective reference in the poem, 'them', seems like the author has confided in the reader; as if the reader should know to what or whom 'them' is referring, though the antecedent is ambiguous.

Ultimately, however, it could be argued that all of the noun phrases in the poem function as targets to describe the initial reference point, 'Words'. In setting up semantic fields, a series of connected metaphors and ambivalent lexical/grammatical choices against this initial reference point, all word choices in this poem become self-reflexive and work to form the subtext of the poem: the emphasis on the longevity, permanence and interpretation of the written word. It is clear that 'Words' invites readers to think reflectively on the nature of words: their ambivalence, their power and their endurance.

4.7 Further activities

1.

Text 4I is a list of noun phrases that occur in the opening pages of Ian McEwan's *Enduring Love*. The novel begins with the narrator, Joe Rose, describing – in great detail – a hot air balloon incident. All of the noun phrases listed below refer to this particular event. As observed in Figures 3.1 and 3.2 in Chapter 3, the arrows here represent elaborative relationships, which are established in this passage when the noun phrase has been mentioned more than once within the same sentence.

Text 4I

the beginning
the moment → the pinprick on the time map
the danger → it
the scene
the colossus
the encounter → it
the event → – the fall – → what happened in a field waiting for its early summer mowing
a balloon → an enormous balloon filled with helium
a catastrophe

1   Identify the kinds of determiners used in each construction. How do they vary throughout the scene? What is the stylistic effect of this variation?

2   Of course, all of these examples profile noun schemas. What do you notice about the conceptual bases of these profiles?

3   Are there any connections between these noun phrases? Does one elaborate on another?

2.

Text 4J below is the opening of Harriet Lane's contemporary thriller novel *Her*, and is centred on the character, Nina, who begins stalking another woman, Emma.

Text 4J

It's her. I'm almost sure of it.

It's late afternoon, a Friday towards the end of July. I've just left the off-licence with a cold bottle wrapped up in paper, and I'm crossing the square, thinking about the afternoon's work, whether I'm getting anywhere or whether it's going to be yet another dead end. The sky, through the shifting canopy of plane leaves, is still saturated with heat, and the golden air is viscous with pollen; but it's tainted, too, with the disquieting scent of the urban summer: the reek of exhausts and drains and sewers, the faraway stench of the ancient forgotten streams that seep through the rocks and silt deep beneath my feet.

I'm thinking about that exact shade of violet – wondering if I've got it quite right against the greens and muddy browns – when I see her. She's on the other side of the square, stooping a little, reaching out to a toddler. The sensation of it, of finding her there in front of me after all this time, is almost overwhelmingly powerful: like panic, or passion. I feel my hands curl into fists. I'm very conscious now of my lungs filling with air, and then releasing it.

I walk away across the square, not looking back … and I'm thinking: *Emma. It's you. I've found you.* And when I pay for the bread and cheese at the deli, my hands are trembling, just a little.

(Lane 2014: 1)

1   How are reference points used to guide the reader's attention in this scene?

2   What kinds of verb profiles are used here?

a   Do we scan the actions of the narrator summatively or sequentially?

b   How does this change across the scene?

3   Finally, connect these ideas to the character's perspective. How is point of view represented in this text? What does this tell us about Nina's character?

3.

The next chapter considers larger units of language: clauses. Based on what you already know about how cognitive grammar categorizes smaller units of language, can you make any predictions about its treatment of larger linguistic constructions?

4.8 Further reading

The key roles of nouns and verbs in cognitive grammar are addressed in Langacker (2008). For another overview of the concepts introduced in this chapter, see the early chapters in Taylor (2002). The analogy of watching a film versus viewing a multi-exposure photograph to explain differences in scanning is taken from Langacker (2008: 109–11). A succinct account of the ideas presented in this chapter is provided in the introduction to Littlemore and Taylor (2014). This edited collection brings together work from researchers across the field of cognitive linguistics, and provides an accessible yet comprehensive overview of some of the more central cognitive grammar claims, including how nouns, verbs and reference points are treated in cognitive grammar (see Bennett 2014, in particular). For a critical view on summary and sequence scanning, see Broccias and Hollman (2007). In stylistics, the role of profiling in literary contexts has begun to be explored, particularly in relation to poetry: see, for example, Hamilton (2003) – the first application of cognitive grammar in a stylistic context. For other applications of cognitive grammar to poetry, see also Stockwell (2009) and Neary (2014). The role of reference point relationships in literature is another area of cognitive grammar for stylistics that has invited some exploratory research (see Stockwell 2009). Additionally, Van Vliet (2009) explores how reference points function in larger stretches of discourse, and touches upon Text World Theory (Werth 1999; Gavins 2007) to help scaffold these concepts. Another paper that considers the role of scanning, but within a literary linguistic context, is Nuttall (2014). Additionally, Harrison (2017b) questions the role scanning plays in the stylistic representation of flashbacks and memory loss.

Note

1   N.B. that perfective and imperfective verb schemas in cognitive grammar refer to two basic subclasses of verb, and are not used to refer to verb tense in this context.

Chapter 5
Clauses

Key objectives

In this chapter we will explore:

- what clauses are and how they are organized in cognitive grammar;
- how clauses can be categorized according to voice and the number of participants involved;
- how verb choices and the relationships between participants and processes can be described and experienced in terms of energy and motion;
- the relationships between clauses in the construction of sentences; and
- the relationships across sentences in the construction of textual cohesion.

5.1 Fictive simulation and clauses

Clauses are important in cognitive terms as they are our basic means of understanding, describing and interacting with the world around us, and therefore play a key role in how we represent experience.

Generally speaking, clauses are units of language that are headed by a verb process. Usually, an entity – a nominal – performs or is acted upon by that process. In isolation, and without wider context, words arguably do not function to communicate much more than their semantic meaning. The simple act of stringing together a participant and a verb, however, gives further meaning to any utterance. Consider, for example, the following two nouns:

- cake
- Chloe

Here, we can attach prototypical definitions to the two words: cake = a food item usually made of flour, eggs and sugar; Chloe = a proper noun, typically used as a name for a female person. By adding a verb in combination with these nominals, however, a specific event is described:

- Chloe eats cake

Very simply, such a sentence includes a participant ('Chloe') who is carrying out a process ('eats'), and another participant which is on the receiving end of the action ('cake'). Though this example has two participants, the number of participants can vary from clause to clause. Sometimes only one participant is present ('*Chloe* is eating') and at other times more than one participant, or more than one verb, can be included ('*Chloe* uses *the fork* to eat *the cake*'). In grammar, this depends on whether the verb is represented as a **transitive, intransitive** or **ditransitive** context. This is discussed in further detail in Section 5.6.2.

Taken in context, we can verify that this is a communication of an event that actually took place, and many readers of this book will be able to relate to such an experience and therefore mentally simulate the real-world event of eating cake. Of course, within the context of literature, however, clauses act to replicate real-world experiences but they also have the potential to communicate events that have not necessarily taken place, or that readers have not directly experienced.

- The cake eats Chloe

While we can imagine both the process and the participants involved in eating cake, our conceptualization of a sentence like 'The cake eats Chloe' is based on what is known in cognitive grammar as **fictive simulation**. We are also able to imagine this event, and to activate knowledge that will allow us to mentally picture this occurrence. When we read books and texts, this process happens all the time – albeit with scenarios that are not necessarily so nightmarish!

5.1.1 Clause creation and asymmetry

The example of fictive simulation above was generated through inverting the grammatical roles of the participants in the sentence. The fact that this describes an entirely new sentence exemplifies role asymmetry in language. In other words, swapping around subject and object yields an entirely new meaning: for example, 'the athlete threw the javelin' is a different scenario than 'the javelin threw the athlete'.

This asymmetry is distinguished from prominence asymmetry brought about by alternate construals of the same conceptual content. For example, unlike the pair of sentences just mentioned, 'the athlete threw the javelin' and 'the javelin was thrown by the athlete' do describe the same conceptual content – the same scene – it is just that in these clauses, the emphasis is altered: the javelin and athlete are alternately given more and less prominence. This alteration of construal is brought about by changing the **voice** of the clause (considered in greater detail in Section 5.6.1).

5.1.2 Prototypical clause constructions

In cognitive grammar, clauses are said to have a **default viewing arrangement**. This describes the idea that clauses are made prototypically by two speakers, in the same location, who are discussing or commenting on their surroundings or what is happening around them. The easiest way to think about this default arrangement is to imagine a spoken exchange between two discourse participants, as in Text 5A.

Text 5A

Jack: How can you sit there, calmly eating muffins when we are in this horrible trouble, I can't make out. You seem to me to be perfectly heartless.

Algernon: Well, I can't eat muffins in an agitated manner. The butter would probably get on my cuffs. One should always eat muffins quite calmly. It is the only way to eat them.

Jack: I say it's perfectly heartless you're eating muffins at all, under the circumstances

Algernon: When I am in trouble, eating is the only thing that consoles me. Indeed, when I am in really great trouble, as any one who knows me intimately will tell you, I refuse everything except food and drink. At the present moment I am eating muffins because I am unhappy. Besides, I am particularly fond of muffins. [*Rising*]

Jack: [*Rising*] Well, that is no reason why you should eat them all in that greedy way. [*Takes muffins from Algernon.*]

Algernon: [*Offering tea-cake*] I wish you would have tea-cake instead. I don't like tea-cake.

(Wilde 1898 [1999]: 69)

In this extract, two of the central characters, Jack and Algernon, are sitting in a garden eating muffins and teacakes – and commenting on the act of doing so. Much of their exchange is concerned with the events that are happening around them and expressing their thoughts ('At the present moment I am eating muffins because I am unhappy'). In fact it is the very immediacy of this commentary – that Jack and Algernon are arguing over muffins and tea-cakes rather than their respective romantic turmoils going on at the time in the play – which generates the humour in this scene.

In spoken discourse contexts, this default arrangement seems a logical one. It is clear to see why drawing together words to make a clause enables us to communicate our experience of the world with others. In reading, however, the default arrangement is arguably more complicated than this. In any given fictional world scenario there is a narrator or focalizer who directly or indirectly addresses another character or an implied addressee. At the same time, there is a writer behind the language choices of the narrator, and a reader who similarly plays an essential part in this exchange.

While the default viewing arrangement describes the typical situation in which clauses are produced, in cognitive grammar the canonical-event model describes the archetypal relationship between nouns and verbs within the clause itself; what we think of as the characteristic subject-verb-object format of clauses in English. This event model describes an agent who carries out an action, and a patient that undergoes a change of some kind.

These two prototypical arrangements can be represented as in Figures 5.1 and 5.2 below:

Figure 5.1 The default viewing arrangement

Figure 5.2 The canonical-event model

Figure 5.1 demonstrates the default viewing arrangement. In this scene, there are two discourse participants who are communicating about their immediate and current environment (i.e. commenting on the cake in front of them).

In Figure 5.2, the canonical-event model is outlined. Here, there is an off-stage viewer (the surprised stick-man who observes the scene) and there is a clear agent (the cake) who is performing an action (chasing), and a second participant, or patient, who is being chased.

5.2 Clause types

In order to successfully communicate with those around us, we need to be able to use appropriate constructions in given contexts. It is therefore helpful that we have flexibility regarding how we can portray or construe a particular event. In English there are a number of clausal constructions at our disposal. These options mean that we are able to accurately capture particular events or simulated events in language, and consequently to express differences in emphasis and prominence.

Following the prototypical structures introduced in the previous section about how clauses are viewed and structured, it is also helpful to think about clauses schematically. As mentioned, a clause is headed by a verb. Consequently, thinking about the type of process described by the verb is a useful starting point. Broadly speaking, there are three general clause types that we can identify.

Table 5.1 Clause types: stative, dynamic and cognitive

Stative	Stative clauses describe a situation in which no energy is created or exchanged between entities. Such clauses simply illustrate a state of affairs that exists or continues. Stative clauses can describe one entity in terms of another ('The vase sits on the table'), can provide further identifying information about an entity ('Luke, I am your father') or can outline the particular attributes of an entity ('The narrative is action-packed').
Dynamic	In contrast to stative clauses, dynamic clauses describe something that happens. The simplest way of thinking about these clauses is to consider verbs of movement ('Richard Parker jumped into the boat') or action ('I drank my gingerbeer').
Cognitive	Cognitive clauses are those that designate a verb of cognition or perception (e.g. 'She enjoyed her holiday', 'I heard the news', 'He understood the repercussions').

Activity 5.1: Setting the scene

Text 5B is a short extract from the opening to Neil Gaiman's novella *Coraline*.

Text 5B

Coraline discovered the door a little while after they moved into the house.

It was a very old house – it had an attic under the roof and a cellar under the ground and an overgrown garden with huge old trees in it.

Coraline's family didn't own all of the house, it was too big for that. Instead they owned part of it.

There were other people who lived in the old house.

Miss Spink and Miss Forcible lived in the flat below Coraline's, on the ground floor. They were both old and round, and they lived in their flat with a number of ageing highland terriers who had names like Hamish and Andrew and Jock.

(Gaiman 2002: 1)

1   Identify which clauses in the extract are stative, dynamic or cognitive.

2   Which clause-type predominates? What is the effect of this?

5.2.1 Intransitive versus transitive clauses

Clauses can involve one participant (intransitive), two participants (transitive) or three participants (ditransitive), as in the examples in Table 5.2.

The distinction between these categories depends on what function the verbs perform within the context of the clause. In other words, while some verbs can be used with a single participant (such as 'roared'), in other contexts the same verb could be used with two participants ('*The lion* roared at *the man*').

It is also important to remember that in order for an entity to be a participant in a clause, it needs to be involved as a central or essential part of the clause, and not simply extra information that can be removed without altering the meaning. For example, the sentence 'Coraline discovered the door' is a transitive clause as there are two participants present – 'Coraline' and 'the door'. (N.B. A verb such as 'discovered' is always used transitively, as it would not provide enough meaning if used intransitively: e.g. 'Coraline discovered' is an incomplete construction.) At the same time, a sentence like 'Coraline discovered the door at night' is still categorized as a transitive clause. Although there is an additional preposition phrase with an embedded noun phrase ('at night'), this is not a participant that is affected or involved in the verb process: it simply provides further information about when the action takes place.

5.2.2 Voice

In cognitive grammar, subjects in clauses are based on focal prominence rather than any content-based definition. In other words, in other clauses as well as those with verbs of cognition, the subject is either the agent or the most 'agent-like' thing within the construction. Cognitive grammar identifies a clausal agent as the **primary focal participant** (i.e. the participant that receives the greatest attention) and the patient as a **secondary focal participant**.

Table 5.2 Clausal participants

Intransitive	*The storm* raged.
	The lion roared.
Transitive	*I* don't like *teacake*.
	Coraline discovered *the door*.
Ditransitive	*The student* emailed *her assignment* to *the tutor*.
	The teacher read *the children a story*.

This is helpful in the creation of clauses, as it allows us to attribute greater or lesser attention to particular parts of a sentence, depending on which entities we want to emphasize. However, when the **voice** of the clause is altered, the relationship between the primary and secondary focal participants becomes disrupted. Providing an alternate construal of the same event often means creating a passive construction (see Chapter 3), where a participant that would otherwise be a landmark instead becomes a trajector.

Consider, for example, the following two sentences:

- The surgeon performs the operation. (Active voice)
- The operation is being performed by the surgeon. (Passive voice)

In both sentences, the same scene is described, but the trajectory is represented differently. The surgeon is carrying out the action in both sentences, and is therefore the agent within each clause, but while the 'surgeon' is also the primary focal participant in the first sentence, he or she is attentionally downgraded in the second. What happens in this alternate construal, and in clauses that are presented in the passive voice more generally, is that the represented motion is removed. Passives therefore remove focus from the agent; placing more emphasis on the patient and consequently adjusting our construal of the activity that has taken place.

5.3 Action chains and archetypal roles

Cognitive grammar similarly provides a model that allows linguists to analyse clause structure systematically. Unlike the transitivity system (see recommended reading in Section 5.7), however, a cognitive grammar account of the relationship between verbs and nouns in clauses is premised on the idea of motion and energy.

Let us consider how this works by using a metaphor of a billiard-ball table. In a game of billiards, one ball is moved and hits another, which in turn comes into physical contact with another, and so on. Within the context of grammar, this is called an **action chain**. It is helpful to think of actions in language as performing a prototypical or **archetypal role** within a clause. There are six main archetypal roles within the cognitive grammar model, but let us start with the two most straightforward archetypal roles:

- **Agent** (energy source): a clausal participant that (wilfully) initiates an action.
- **Patient** (energy sink): a participant that goes through a change of some kind.

To put these examples within the context of the billiard-ball model, the agent would be the person playing who operates the cue. The agent carries out the action, and therefore is known as the **energy source**. At the other end of the action chain is the patient: the billiard ball that was hit by the cue. Since this receives the energy and is affected by it, it can also be described as the **energy sink**.

The billiard cue itself is an **instrument** – the third archetypal role – which describes the entity within a clause that is used by one participant to affect another. Usually, this is an inanimate object. In contrast, an **experiencer** – the fourth archetypal role – is usually a person or at least a sentient entity of some kind. An experiencer in a clause is a participant who, as the name suggests, experiences something. This role is therefore categorized by verbs of perception or cognition, or by a mental or emotive process. Again, within the context of the billiard-ball metaphor, this would be an onlooker or member of the audience, perhaps.

The fifth archetypal role is a **mover**, which quite simply is any entity, animate or inanimate, that physically changes position or location. Finally, the sixth role is the **zero** role, which describes an entity that inhabits a static location. The billiard-ball table itself, for example, would fall into this category.

An additional role, which does not play such an essential part in an action chain, but instead simply provides additional information about where the action occurs, is a **locative**. For example, in a sentence like 'the ball fell from the table to the floor' the ball is a mover, and the constructions 'from the table' and 'to the floor' are locatives that indicate where the action takes place, from the source of the event ('the table') to the goal ('the floor'). At the same time, these pieces of information are not essential – we could remove them from the sentence and still have an understanding of the motion event: 'the ball fell'. Any additional information that describes the time or manner in which the process takes place are called **circumstances**. For example, 'the ball fell *heavily* to the floor'.

Activity 5.2: Identifying roles

Label the role types performed by the penguins/other entities, represented in Figure 5.3, in the following sentences:

1 The penguin runs away.
2 The penguin is asleep.
3 The penguin quickly passes the egg to another penguin.
4 The penguin feels cold.

Figure 5.3 Archetypal roles

5.3.1 Verbs of cognition

The label 'action chain' naturally lends itself well to physical processes, but what about verbs of cognition/perception? The metaphor of the billiard-ball table helps to explain action chain between agent and patient, but in clauses which include verbs of cognition, this idea of energy transfer is a little more complicated.

In such clauses, usually there is a stimulus and an experiencer. Instead of a path of energy or motion, there is a perceptual path between one entity and the next. In other words, the two grammatical participants are still connected together in some way, but in these examples, rather than a transferral of energy, mental contact between one entity and another is established instead.

Agent-like properties can be given to either stimulus or experiencer, though, as the following two alternate construals demonstrate:

- *The bad news* (stimulus) affected *everyone* (experiencer).
- *Everyone* (experiencer) was affected by *the bad news* (stimulus).

In the first sentence, 'the bad news' is the stimulus – the entity that seemingly initiates the event; or, at the very least we might say this is at the head, the start, of the perceptual path. In the second sentence, this is downgraded attentionally: it remains the grammatical participant that initiates the action, but is attentionally less important and secondary to the experiencer itself – 'everyone'. So while conceptually different from the 'motion' or 'energy' transfer more central to dynamic clauses, clauses of cognition can be seen to behave in a similar way to other clause types, with greater or lesser attention/agency assigned to various participants, and similarly affected through alterations in voice, and so on.

Activity 5.3: Roles in headlines

Having introduced these roles within the context of the billiard-ball table metaphor, let us now think about how these prototypical roles work in context. Text 5C below shows some sentences taken from various online news articles.

Text 5C

a *UK election results* have delayed *Brexit talks.*

b *Mervyn Wheatley* wrecked *his yacht* in a hurricane force gale and was rescued by *the Queen Mary 2.*

c *The concert* that heartened and cheered *the nation.*

d *Lewis Hamilton* is the winner once again.

For each clause, identify the archetypal roles represented by the participants (in italics). Where sentences contain more than one clause, please note that a participant might have more than one role.

Activity 5.4: Movement in texts

Looking at individual sentences in isolation is an easy place to start, but of course the texts that we read and the examples of language we encounter in the world tend to be more complicated!

Text 5D shows short extracts from three texts.

Text 5D

a Drips from the roof are plopping into the water-butt by the back door. The view through the windows above the sink is excessively drear. Beyond the dank garden in the courtyard are the ruined walls on the edge of the moat. Beyond the moat, the boggy ploughed fields stretch to the leaden sky. I tell myself that all the rain we have had lately is good for nature, and that at any moment spring will surge on us.

I Capture the Castle (Smith 1949: 7)

b The stars are tiny specks of light in the darkness. Unlike the planets, they exhibit no extravagant loops on the sky, and, for the overwhelming majority of them, we have no telescope capable of resolving any detail on their surfaces. Beyond the nightly circular arcs across the sky induced by the Earth's spin, they appear to be immobile, featureless points. And yet we know the distance to each and every one.

Universal: A Guide to the Cosmos (Cox and Forshaw 2016: 76)

c When I got home from school Father was still out at work, so I unlocked the front door and went inside and took my coat off. I went into the kitchen and put my things on the table. And one of the things was this book which I had taken into school to show to Siobhan. I made myself a raspberry milkshake and heated it up in the microwave and then went through to the living room to watch one of the Blue Planet videos about life in the deepest parts of the ocean.

The Curious Incident of the Dog in the Night-Time (Haddon 2003: 100)

1   Now that you are more familiar with the terminology, again identify the archetypal roles represented by the participants in each clause. If you are stuck or finding it difficult where to start, think about your overall impressions of each passage.

2   Does there seem to be much movement, or is it quite still?

3   Where motion or energy is attributed, is the participant an animate of inanimate entity?

4   Is any extra information provided regarding how, when or where the actions take place?

5.4 Action and inaction

Activity 5.4 helped us to think a little bit about the relationship between action and inaction, and about how the semantic profile of the verb choice, in particular, can either create or remove energy from a sentence or, cumulatively, from a scene overall.

In addition to the semantic associations attributed to particular verb choices, in cognitive grammar another 'slowing factor' that can impact on pace or represented motion is the presence of **modality**. Introduced in greater detail in Chapter 6, modality refers to the ways in which we can create subjectivity in language. Consequently, the presence or inclusion of modality can draw attention away from the scene being described and instead direct it towards the speaker or conceptualizer of that scene – thus creating a more subjective construal (see Chapter 3). This is because modality is seen to have a kind of latent or deferred energy.

If we think about when we add modals to verbs of action, for example, we can take away the force or urgency attached to that verb choice:

- I sprinted across the park vs. I could have sprinted across the park.
- The driver slammed on the brakes vs. The driver definitely slammed on the brakes.
- The plane accelerated down the runway vs. The plane must have accelerated down the runway.

When modality is added ('could', 'definitely', 'must'), the force of motion presented is lessened in some way. This either happens by creating a hypothetical, unrealized scenario ('I could have sprinted across the park'), or by interrupting the sense of validity or certainty of the statement. While both 'definitely' and 'must' display high epistemic certainty, for example, their subjectivity conversely casts doubt on the statement made by the speaker. In other words, an unmodalized, categorical assertion explicitly describes the action, whereas the modalized version problematizes the existence of the motion event.

To think about how this works in a little more detail stylistically, let us consider Text 5E. In Patrick Ness' novel *A Monster Calls*, a young boy, Conor, is visited by a monster who tells him three tales. The story is about coping with grief and loss, and many reviewers argue that the visits of 'the monster' are a metaphor for these emotions. There are many occasions in the novel where the monster and Conor's role become conflated and blurred, to the extent that many of Conor's actions are attributed to the monster, and vice versa – and this can be observed in the representation of action chains and modality in this scene.

Text 5E

Conor could feel the monster close behind him, knew that it was kneeling, knew that it was putting its face up to his ear to whisper into it, to tell him the rest of the story.

He called, it said, *for a **monster***.

And it reached a huge, monstrous hand past Conor and knocked Harry flying across the floor.

Trays clattered and people screamed as Harry tumbled past them. Anton and Sully looked aghast, first at Harry, then back at Conor.

Their faces changed as they saw him. Conor took another step towards them, feeling the monster towering behind him.

Anton and Sully turned and ran.

(Ness 2011: 176–7. Emphases as original)

In this short extract, Conor and the monster are facing some bullies from Conor's school in the canteen at lunchtime. The extract starts with casting Conor in the role of the experiencer and the monster as the stimulus, but the verb profiles that designate these archetypal roles simultaneously foreground Conor's subjective construal. Conor 'could feel the monster close behind him' and 'knew' particular facts: that 'it was kneeling' and 'putting its face up to his ear to whisper into it'.

The extract then shifts to provide a more objective construal of events, and the monster takes on a more definitive agent role: 'And it reached a huge, monstrous hand past Conor and knocked Harry flying across the floor.' This sentence first casts the monster as an agent ('it reached'), and then zooms in to foreground 'a huge, monstrous hand' as the instrument that 'knocked Harry flying across the floor'. The assignment of agency here works in an interesting way; the 'huge, monstrous hand' is introduced with an indefinite determiner 'a', which grounds it less specifically. Equally, Conor is included in the clause as reference point in the location of events, but it construed as separate from the action.

The rest of the passage includes a combination of clause roles. Following Harry's attack, there are a few noises that create stimulus/experiencer clauses ('Trays clattered and people screamed'), and the other bullies assume mover roles to escape the monster/Conor ('Anton and Sully turned and ran'). Before they run, however, the narrative describes their reaction to Conor/the monster: 'Their faces changed as they saw him'. Like with the description of the monster's hand before, this is another example of metonymic agency: their 'faces' assume the agent role in the action. Again, it is interesting that there is ambiguity regarding the cause of their reaction – 'Their faces changed as they saw him', but Conor informs us that he is 'feeling the monster towering behind him' at this moment, too. The subjectivity invited by the modality here ('feeling') casts Conor in an experiencer role, and simply makes us question: what are the boys seeing, exactly?

In summary, it is the combination of modality and objectivity in this scene that simultaneously both absolves and implicates Conor's agency in these events. Aside from one agent role ('Conor took another step'), Conor is only explicitly cast in experiencer ('could feel', 'knew', 'feeling') and stimulus ('they saw him') or patient roles ('to tell him') – but at the same time the modality ('could feel', 'knew', 'feeling') means that these events are grounded through his perspective, and therefore that he is not entirely absent from these actions. This displacement and deferral of agency of Conor's part makes it seem as though these actions are outside of his control: initiated by the monster – his grief – and are not a result of his own volition.

Activity 5.5: Action in dystopian fiction

We have briefly considered how modality and subjectivity in language can impact on, and possibly detract from, the force of motion in texts.

Text 5F below is an extract from Suzanne Collins' dystopian novel *The Hunger Games*. Based on the narrative of the novel and film *Battle Royale*, this novel depicts a future society where members from particular districts are nominated, at random, as 'tributes', and are forced to fight to the death in a vast arena. This is known as the 'hunger games', which takes place every year and which is televised to the nation. The narrative is focalized through the first-person perspective of the character Katniss, and this scene depicts the very beginning of the 'games', where all tributes have just entered the arena. Some provisions have been placed in front of them, and they need to make the decision whether to retrieve items that might aid survival or to run and hide. A countdown has indicated that the games have just begun.

Text 5F

And I've missed it! I've missed my chance! Because those extra couple of seconds I've lost by not being ready are enough to change my mind about going in. My feet shuffle for a moment, confused at the direction my brain wants to take, and then I lunge forward, scoop up the sheet of plastic and a loaf of bread. The pickings are so small and I'm so angry with Peeta for distracting me that I sprint in twenty metres to retrieve a bright orange backpack that could hold anything because I can't stand leaving with virtually nothing.

A boy, I think from District 9, reaches the pack at the same time I do and we grapple for it and then he coughs, splattering my face with blood. I stagger back, repulsed by the warm, sticky spray. Then the boy slips to the ground. That's when I see the knife in his back. Already other tributes have reached the Cornucopia and are spreading out to attack. Yes, the girl from District 2, ten metres away, running towards me, one hand clutching a half-dozen knives. I've seen her throw in training. She never misses. And I'm her next target.

All the general fear I've been feeling condenses into an immediate fear of this girl, this predator who might kill me in seconds. Adrenaline shoots through me and I sling the pack over one shoulder and run full-speed for the woods. I can hear the blade whistling towards me and reflexively hike the pack up to protect my head. The blade lodges in the pack. Both straps on my shoulders now, I make for the trees. Somehow I know the girl will not pursue me. That she'll be drawn back into the Cornucopia before all the good stuff is gone. A grin crosses my face. *Thanks for the knife*, I think.

(Collins 2008: 150)

Drawing together the key ideas introduced in this chapter so far, have a think about the stylistic significance of the representation of action chains and clause structures in the above extract.

Use the questions below to help guide your discussion:

1 Which style choices increase the pace of the clauses?

2 Which style choices stall the pace of motion in the clauses?

3 Are the clauses construed objectively or subjectively? Is there a shift between the two types across the extract?

5.5 Building sentences

So far this chapter has observed how clauses can be structured and how action chains can be represented in language. While the focus of this chapter is on building clauses, it may also be helpful at this stage to consider how cognitive grammar approaches constructions of language at the level of the sentence, in particular – or, rather, how clauses can be connected together in order to create larger units of language (see also Chapter 7). In order to consider sentence constructions, the next section briefly returns to a couple of key ideas already introduced in this book, such as the reference point model and profiling.

5.5.1 Subordination and coordination

Some sentences can be formed of one clause, as in the first sentence below:

- I climbed into bed.

On its own, this clause functions successfully as a complete sentence. There is one transitive action ('climbed'), an agent who performs the action ('I') and a patient that receives the action ('bed'). When two or more clauses are joined using a coordinating conjunction (*and*, *but*, *or*, etc.), this creates a coordination of clauses, as in the second sentence below:

- I climbed into bed *and* pulled the covers over my head.

Here, two actions are profiled, as both clauses ('climbed into bed' and 'pulled the covers over my head') are syntactically paralleled and therefore hold equal attention in the sentence. Consequently, in cognitive grammar coordinating sentences are said to represent symmetrical relationships, which we understand by mentally juxtaposing the two (or more) clausal components. This act of mental juxtaposition can invite readers to construe causal or sequential relationships between actions, an idea that is returned to in Section 5.5.2.

If a clause can function as a sentence in its own right, like the first example above, this is known as a main clause. In contrast, a subordinate clause is one that cannot function on its own as a sentence, but instead is dependent on a main clause in order to be understood – either in terms of identifying the subject or in determining the nominal or clausal grounding (see Chapter 6) of a particular phrase. Subordinating conjunctions (*while, because, although, before*) can signpost a subordinate clause (as in the second example below), but are not always used:

- They advised him (to leave the party immediately).
- She injured herself (*while* running).
- The shampoo (you gave me) smells amazing.

Unlike a coordinated sentence where prominence is given to both clauses in equal measure, in a subordinated sentence an asymmetrical relationship is instead represented. In other words, the main clause is profiled, whereas the subordinate clause becomes backgrounded. In each of the sentences above, which represent the three types of subordinate clauses (complement, adverbial and relative, respectively), attention is paid to one of the processes more prominently than the other. In other words, the acts of being advised, of being injured and the smell of the shampoo are profiled, whereas the acts of leaving the party (sentence 1), running (sentence 2) and giving (sentence 3) are not. Subordinating clauses like this can also alter the way in which we construe the grammatical category of the clause. In the second sentence, for example, the adverbial clause 'while running' acts more like a nominalization than an active process and therefore seems to simply offer more description for the process in the main clause.

5.5.2 Textual cohesion

In order for any stylistic tool to work successfully, it needs to be able to describe patterns of language at the level of the sentence and above. While we hope that many of the example analyses in this book demonstrate cognitive grammar's capacity for the sentence-level analysis of texts, cognitive grammar's reference point model (see Chapter 4) is a particularly useful way to explore how texts can build cohesive connections between and across sentences. Consider, for example, Text 5G, the final two paragraphs of *The Great Gatsby*.

Text 5G

And as I sat there brooding on the old, unknown world, I thought of Gatsby's wonder when he first picked out the green light at the end of Daisy's dock. He had come a long way to this blue lawn and his dream must have seemed so close that he could hardly fail to grasp it. He did not know that it was already behind him, somewhere back in that vast obscurity beyond the city, where the dark fields of the republic rolled on under the night.

Gatsby believed in the green light, the orgastic future that year by year recedes before us. It eluded us then, but that's no matter – tomorrow we will run faster, stretch out our arms farther ... . And then one fine morning – So we beat on, boats against the current, borne back ceaselessly into the past.

(Fitzgerald ([1922] 2002): 180)

Text 5G manages to be cohesive in that it maintains connections within and across the sentence boundaries. It also maintains a symmetrical relationship with the paragraph that precedes this extract, which is initiated through the additive conjunction 'and' that begins the first sentence. The textual cohesion is established through several reference points that are prominent parts of the fictional world, and that are reinstated across the extract. The speaking 'I' of the narrator Nick Carraway, for example, is referenced more than once as the agent ('*I* sat') and experiencer ('*I* thought') of two clauses, whereas Gatsby is also referenced multiple times, both nominally in a possessive construction ('*Gatsby's* wonder') and in an experiencer role ('*Gatsby* believed'), and through pronoun substitution ('*He* had come', '*He* did not know'). Nick Carraway famously holds both an observer and a participant role in *The Great Gatsby*, and this is also apparent in the reference point relationships across this extract. While there are reference points to denote himself and his detached 'brooding' speculation on events, much of this extract is Carraway imagining Gatsby's perspective, as well as imagining collective agents: 'before *us*', 'it eluded *us*', '*we* will run', '*we* beat on'.

As well as the reinstatement of these reference points, parallels are also drawn between the descriptions of physical locations and actions in this extract and their corresponding metaphorical locations and actions in other clauses. For example, Carraway describes how Gatsby's dream 'was already behind him, somewhere back in that vast obscurity beyond the city'; and he also describes the 'orgastic future' as a location that can be reached through physical actions if we 'run faster, stretch out our arms farther'. Further parallels are also created across clauses through reconstruals in the language. In the second paragraph, for instance, Carraway talks about 'the green light', but then immediately reconstrues this as 'the orgastic future that year by year recedes before us'. Of course, readers of the novel will be aware the green light is a reference point across the entire novel, acting as a symbol for Gatsby's hopes and desires. The fact that this reconstrual occurs across two clauses within the same sentence acts to profile the various interpretations of this motif, and thus makes the green light's metaphorical role immediately explicit.

In summary, a good starting point for any cognitive grammar analysis that explores the connections between clauses is to consider the reference point relationships in the text, and whether particular constructions – clauses or descriptions that denote locations, characters, objects or themes – are reinstated or repaired across a paragraph, or even the text, as a whole.

5.6 Extended example analysis: Action chains in the Red Wedding scene in *A Storm of Swords*

The final example draws together the ideas introduced in this chapter to present an analysis of the notorious 'Red Wedding' scene from book 3 *A Storm of Swords*, in the *Game of Thrones* series. *Game of Thrones* is a bestselling contemporary fantasy series that has recently been adapted into a TV show by HBO, and which has a reputation for killing off central characters at a moment's notice. This particular scene follows two characters in the Stark family, Catelyn and her son Robb. They attend a wedding of one of Lord Walder Frey's daughters, Roslin, whom Robb was originally supposed to marry. Since the Starks reneged on their promise, Frey disguises his soldiers as musicians and plots to kill the Starks at the wedding. Just before this scene, explicit negation works to foreshadow the events to come: Catelyn notes how 'a wedding feast was not a battle, but there were always dangers when men were in their cups' (Martin 2000: 124) – but a one-sided battle is what ensues. Though Text 5H is only a brief passage from the text, it is exemplary of the style patterns across the chapter as a whole. The scene unfolds slowly, and with increasingly building tension, before the final bloody and action-filled climax.

Text 5H

The drums were pounding again, pounding and pounding and pounding.
   Dacey Mormont, who seemed to be the only woman left in the hall besides Catelyn, stepped up behind Edwyn Frey, and touched him lightly on the arm as she said something in his ear. Edwyn wrenched himself away from her with unseemly violence. 'No', he said, too loudly. 'I'm done with dancing for the nonce'. Dacey paled and turned away. Catelyn got slowly to her feet. *What just happened there?* Doubt gripped her heart, where an instant before had been only weariness. *It is nothing*, she tried to tell herself, *you are seeing grumkins in the woodpile, you are become an old*

silly woman sick with grief and fear. But something must have shown on her face. Even Ser Wendel Manderly took note. 'Is something amiss?' he asked, the leg of lamb in his hands.

She did not answer him. Instead she went after Edwyn Frey. The players in the gallery had finally gotten both king and queen down to their name-day suits. With scarcely a moment's respite, they began to play a very different sort of song. No one sang the words, but Catelyn knew 'The Rains of Castamere' when she heard it. Edwyn was hurrying toward a door. She hurried faster, driven by the music. Six quick strides and she caught him. *And who are you, the proud lord said, that I must bow so low?* She grabbed Edwyn by the arm to turn him and went cold all over when she felt the iron rings beneath his silken sleeve.

Catelyn slapped him so hard she broke his lip. *Olyvar*, she thought, *and Perwyn, Alesander, all absent. And Roslin wept.*

Edwyn Frey shoved her aside. The music drowned all other sound, echoing off the walls as if the stones themselves were playing. Robb gave Edwyn an angry look and moved to block his way ... and staggered suddenly as a quarrel sprouted from his side, just beneath the shoulder. If he screamed then, the sound was swallowed by the pipes and horns and fiddles. Catelyn saw a second bolt pierce his leg, saw him fall. Up in the gallery, half the musicians had crossbows in their hands instead of drums or lutes. She ran toward her son, until something punched in the small of the back and the hard stone floor came up to slap her. '*Robb!*' she screamed. She saw Smalljon Umber wrestle a table off its trestles. Crossbow bolts thudded into the wood, one two three, as he flung it down on top of his king. Robin Flint was ringed by Freys, their daggers rising and falling. Ser Wendel Manderly rose ponderously to his feet, holding his leg of lamb. A quarrel went in his open mouth and came out the back of his neck. Ser Wendel crashed forward, knocking the table off its trestles and sending cups, flagons, trenchers, platters, turnips, beets, and wine bouncing, spilling, and sliding across the floor.

Like all chapters in the *Game of Thrones* series, the chapter is focalized through the perspective of a particular character, in this instance Catelyn Stark. Initially, feelings of unease are created through Catelyn's throwaway descriptions of the scene. Before this particular scene, she notes of the bride, for example, that 'Poor Roslin's smile had a fixed quality to it, as if someone had sewn it onto her face' (Martin 2000: 123). This description establishes Roslin, and the Starks by extension, as puppet-like, at the mercy of someone else's control. Equally, the descriptions of the noise and crowds earlier in this chapter build a sense of claustrophobia. Catelyn repeatedly makes references to the noisy music: 'The musicians in the gallery might be numerous and loud, but they were not especially gifted' (Martin 2000: 125), and notes how 'the heat and smoke and noise were making her feel sick' (Martin 2000: 125). The cataloguing of noun profiles here through the use of additive conjunctions ('heat and smoke and noise'), as well as the repeated verb profiles in the description of the drums ('pounding and pounding and pounding') place equal attention on each part of the scene in turn, and the listing of all the noises compounds the overwhelming atmosphere created by the surroundings. The description of the drums, in particular, is repeated throughout and it becomes a motif or a stylistic refrain for the chapter as a whole.

The first paragraph in Text 5H is characterized by modalized descriptions which function to show Catelyn's uncertainty and unease. The representation of Catelyn's thoughts (*'What just happened there?'*) establishes her as external to the scene unfolding around her: She appears to be attempting to reassure herself, and her description of the scene further acts to place her in the role of an observer. From the beginning of the scene, there are modalized descriptions which express her uncertainty explicitly. She shows her experiencer status by describing what 'seemed' to be the case and that 'something must have shown on her face', and ambiguity is also created through low levels of specificity in particular descriptions ('she said something') and the use of rhetorical questions. The word 'something' is itself repeated three times in this first paragraph, representing what is happening in only the vaguest of terms. In Catelyn's recounting of events, Dacey is connected with low-energy mover roles ('stepped up', 'touched him lightly', 'turned away'), which contrast with the construal of Edwyn's more aggressive, and seemingly disproportionate, physical actions: We read how he 'wrenched himself away from her with unseemly violence'. Furthermore, Catelyn's position as an onlooker is expounded by her position as a patient in some clauses; she is at the receiving end of external factors and her own feelings and emotions ('Doubt gripped *her heart*'; and 'she tried to tell *herself*'; 'something must have shown on *her face*').

Fans of the series will be aware that the Rains of Castamere is a cautionary song which functions as a reference point for the onset of danger. In this second paragraph, the music becomes a causal agent, driving Catelyn to hurry 'faster', as the scene describes how she 'caught' and 'grabbed' Edwyn. Her experiencer status does not entirely disappear in this second paragraph, however; she immediately 'knew' the music and recognized what it represents; and she 'felt' the armour beneath Edwyn's wedding attire. As soon as Catelyn does become aware that Edwyn is wearing 'iron rings beneath his silken sleeve', however, the intent of the set-up becomes explicitly apparent to both character and reader. While Catelyn retrospectively comprehends key facts that were mentioned earlier in the scene but not fully understood (*'Olyvar,* she thought, *and Perwyn, Alesander, all absent. And Roslin wept*') there is also a shift to more forceful agent roles ('grabbed', 'slapped', 'broke') as she recognizes the danger they are in and the violence commences.

This second half of the scene is consequently marked by reconstrual of previous events and descriptions ('up in the gallery, half the musicians had crossbows in their hands instead of drums or lutes') as it becomes apparent that the Starks have been set-up. In the final paragraph, the verb choices themselves explicitly profile the domain of violence ('shoved, 'drowned', 'staggered', 'screamed', 'slap', 'fall', 'thudded', 'wrestle', 'ran', 'pierce', 'punched'). Furthermore, agency is frequently given to non-animate entities in this half, which represents Catelyn's confusion and disorientation. It seems as though the attack is happening so quickly she is unsure who is initiating each assault:

- *The music* drowned all other sound, echoing off the walls as if *the stones* themselves were playing.
- The sound was swallowed by *the pipes and horns and fiddles*.
- *The hard stone* floor came up to slap her.
- *Crossbow bolts* thudded into the wood.
- Catelyn saw *a second bolt* pierce his leg.
- *Their daggers* rising and falling.
- *A quarrel* went in to his open mouth and came out the back of his neck.

Furthermore, many of the patients in these clauses are body parts, specifically ('his side', 'his leg', 'the small of the back', 'his open mouth') which act to foreground the physicality and violence in the scene. Equally, the helplessness of Catelyn and Robb's positions are also signposted in the presentation of clauses. Their agency is disrupted by hypothetical frames ('if he screamed') and both their actions are disrupted by other forces: Robb 'moved to block' Edwyn, but 'staggered suddenly' as he is hit by an arrow, while Catelyn 'ran toward her son, until something punched in the small of her back'. In other words, both characters initiate incomplete actions which show the undoubted futility of their attempts to fight back, and, consequently, their vulnerability.

Like with the very first sentence in this extract, prominence is also given to the music and sounds in the latter half of the scene. The music is represented as an agent and the primary focal participant that 'drowned all other sound', and as a secondary participant in the clause that describes how 'the pipes and horns and fiddles' 'swallowed' the sound of Robb's (potential) scream. As mentioned earlier, the cacophony of sounds here arguably contributes to the agitation and turbulence; something which is also utilized and emphasized in the adaptation of this scene for the TV series. The listing of noun profiles ('the pipes and horns and fiddles'; 'cups, flagons, trenchers, platters, turnips, beets, and wine') and verb profiles ('bouncing, spilling and sliding') at the end of this passage contrasts with the underspecified descriptions at the beginning. Again, this overloading of details accentuates the sheer overwhelming nature of the assault.

In summary, the progression of clause structures in this extract builds up a sense of tension and uncertainty in the first half of the passage, while accentuating the violence, turmoil and futility in the second. This stylistic contrast can be explored through a combined account of action chains, role types and modalization, as these patterns of language evidently play a key role in our experience of reading this memorable scene.

5.7 Further activities

1.

Text 5I contains the famous opening paragraphs of Daphne Du Maurier's novel *Rebecca*.

Text 5I

Last night I dreamt I went to Manderley again. It seemed to me I stood by the iron gate leading to the drive, and for a while I could not enter, for the way was barred to me. There was a padlock and chain upon the gate. I called in my dream to the lodge-keeper, and had no answer, and peering closer through the rusted spokes of the gate I saw that the lodge was uninhabited.

No smoke came from the chimney, and the little lattice windows gaped forlorn. Then, like all dreamers, I was possessed of a sudden with supernatural powers and passed like a spirit through the barrier before me. The drive wound away in front of me, twisting and turning as it had always done, but as I advanced I was aware that a change had come upon it; it was narrow and unkempt, not the drive that we had known. At first I was puzzled and did not understand, and it was only when I bent my head to avoid the low swinging branch of a tree that I realized what had happened. Nature had come into her own again and, little by little, in her stealthy, insidious way had encroached upon the drive with long, tenacious fingers. The woods, always a menace even in the past, had triumphed in the end. They crowded, dark and uncontrolled, to the borders of the drive. The beeches with white, naked limbs leant close to one another, their branches intermingled in a strange embrace, making a vault above my head like the archway of a church. And there were other trees as well, trees that I did not recognize, squat oaks and tortured elms that straggled cheek by jowl with the beeches, and had thrust themselves out of the quiet earth, along with monster shrubs and plants, none of which I remembered.

The drive was a ribbon now, a thread of its former self, with gravel surface gone, and choked with grass and moss. The trees had thrown out low branches, making an impediment to progress; the gnarled roots looked like skeleton claws. Scattered here and again amongst this jungle growth I would recognize shrubs that had been landmarks in our time, things of culture and grace, hydrangeas whose blue heads had been famous. No hand had checked their progress, and they had gone native now, rearing to monster height without a bloom, black and ugly as the nameless parasites that grew beside them.

(Du Maurier 1938: 1–2)

Rewrite a section from this following extract by either

1   removing the modality;
2   changing the voice of particular clauses; or
3   altering the action chains in some way: for example, by changing the participant role by profiling a different verb choice; including extra participants (such as instruments, patients) and so on.

Keep a note of the changes you have made and compare your rewritten version with both the original and with a classmate. How do these alterations impact on the way the text is read?

2.

In groups, go online and select a current news story. Find an article on the story from different sources and carry out an analysis of the action chains/ archetypal roles selected in the articles.

1   What do you notice about the way the clauses are structured?
2   Which participants form the primary focus of attention, and to whom is the agency assigned?

To help you consider these questions, you may also want to draw on the ideas of noun/verb profiles and lexical schemas introduced in Chapter 4.

3.

Cognitive grammar's action chain model is frequently compared to Halliday's system of transitivity (see Chapter 1, Section 1.3). Activity 2 above, for example, is a popular grammatical exercise for exploring how agency and blame is attributed in language.

1 In your opinion, what are the similarities between the transitivity and cognitive grammar models for exploring action and clause construction?

2 What are the limitations of each approach?

3 How might an analysis of action chains provide us with new ways of thinking about how action, energy and motion are presented in texts?

5.8 Further reading

Langacker's chapter on clause structure (2008: 354–405) covers the ideas presented here, and provides further detail regarding how clauses are coded. Additionally, his chapter on complex sentences (2008: 413–36) further breaks down the different types of clauses that can exist in sentence structures, in particular. For an accessible overview of how clauses structure in cognitive grammar, see also Taylor (2002: 413–36). Accounts of energy and action can also be found in other cognitive linguistic models. To explore how energy is considered from a cognitive-semantics perspective, for example, see Talmy's (2000a, b) ideas on force dynamics and event frames. Further, the concept of 'defocusing' agents in passive voice constructions was first identified by Shibatani (1985). The ideas for the action chain model was initially suggested by Fillmore (1968), and later expanded on in Langacker (1991). Since Halliday's (1971) groundbreaking paper, analyses of action and agency have been seen as a cornerstone of the field of stylistics. The transitivity system offered by Halliday allowed researchers to categorize the types of verb choices made by writers, and consequently enabled linguists to consider, in a systematic way, the clausal patterns across texts. For stylisticians, this has enabled an even more rigorous analysis of how such patterns can bring about particular stylistic effects. Furthermore, the transitivity system also allowed researchers to consider exactly how agency is performed in texts: who is the initiator of the action, who receives the action and how that action is carried out. If interested in exploring the differences between cognitive grammar and Halliday's transitivity model further, see Halliday (1971; 1973; 1985) and Halliday and Hasan (1976). For a comparison of cognitive grammar and systemic-functional grammar, see Nuttall (2018). The first extended application for cognitive grammar for a stylistic account of action is Stockwell's (2009) analysis, and this is later expanded on in

Stockwell (2014). A more detailed analysis of the ideas presented in Section 5.5 can be found in Chapter 3 in Harrison (2017a), which explores the relationship between action chains and archetypal roles in a text that combines both high energy and ineffective action within the same passage. In addition, Simpson's work (2014b) considers how pace is maintained and disrupted in various stylistic contexts.

Chapter 6
Grounding

Key objectives

In this chapter we will explore:

- the concept of grounding in cognitive grammar;
- how various grounding elements and strategies operate; and
- how cognitive grammar treats different modal forms as clausal grounding elements.

6.1 An introduction to grounding

6.1.1 What is grounding?

Imagine a friend says to you 'lecturer mark assignment'.

In this instance, although the meaning of individual words is clear and you might well have an overall understanding of what your friend is trying to say, something still feels quite unusual about this particular utterance. We can explore this in more detail by thinking about the ambiguities in this expression.

- It is difficult to work out exactly who the lecturer is.
- It is difficult to work out exactly which assignment is being referred to.
- It is difficult to assign some sense of time to action: has the assignment been marked? Is it being marked? Is it about to be marked?

These ambiguities are a result of the stripped-down nature of the utterance; it only contains two nouns 'lecturer' and 'assignment' and a verb 'mark'. Now imagine that this skeletal clause has the following elements (in italics) added to it:

The lecturer mark*ed every* assignment.

Instantly, the utterance becomes easier to comprehend; we now have a particular lecturer mentioned, greater specificity in terms of what was marked and an understanding of when this was done relative to the utterance through the use of the past tense.

To explain why adding these elements leads to a clearer understanding, we will return first of all to the notion of the **ground**. In cognitive grammar, the ground is defined as the context or situation of a discourse event, consisting of the participants (e.g. speaker and hearer), the immediate surrounding physical environment and the time of interaction.

Grounding is the process by which states and events in an utterance are fixed in relation to the current speech event, providing information about what happened, when it happened and who was involved. In our example, the speaker uses the words 'the' and 'every' and the inflected verb form 'marked' in order to direct the hearer's attention to more specific detail. Using **grounding elements** gives a hearer access to particular instances of 'lecturer', 'mark' and 'assignment' rather than simply generic ones, and specifies that the marking of the assignments happened in the past. The use of grounding elements helps to ensure that these instances are conceptualized by the hearer. This shared understanding, necessary for communication to take place, is known as **coordinated mental reference**.

We will explore the different types of grounding elements as we move through this chapter but you will probably have noticed straightaway that nouns and verbs are grounded in different ways. In our example, the noun 'lecturer' is grounded by the definite article 'the'. Equally, the noun 'assignment' is grounded by the determiner 'every'. In both cases, the grounding forms a nominal (the process is called **nominal grounding**): in this instance 'the lecturer' and 'every assignment'. On the other hand, 'mark' is grounded and becomes a finite clause through the use of the past tense bound morpheme –ed.

Activity 6.1: Identifying grounding elements for nouns

Identify the grounding elements for each of the nouns in the following examples. What do you notice? Can you begin to see a pattern in terms of the kinds of words that can function as grounding elements?

1   The bridge was open to traffic.
2   Have you read this book?
3   Some of the players were not happy with the referee's decision.
4   Each customer received a refund.

5   No warning was given.

6   Can I buy you a drink?

6.1.2 Types and instances

We can also understand the difference between 'lecturer' and 'the lecturer' and 'assignment' and 'every assignment' by thinking in more detail about how these particular expressions function.

As we saw in Chapter 4, nouns profile things; in these instances the ungrounded lecturer and assignment are very general, abstract labels that do not identify a particular **referent**. In cognitive grammar, we can therefore say that 'lecturer' and 'assignment' simply specify a type of thing.

In contrast, the grounding elements 'the' and 'every' each help to evoke a particular instance of the types 'lecturer' and 'assignment'. This relationship can be seen in Figure 6.1. Here, the noun 'lecturer' specifies a type of thing with different possible instances. The grounded nominal 'The lecturer' in the first shaded circle is an instance of that type; the grounding element 'The' diverts the hearer's attention to a specific instance. The definite article 'The' allows the speaker and hearer access to a referent that will be identifiable within the ground.

Figure 6.1 Type and instance

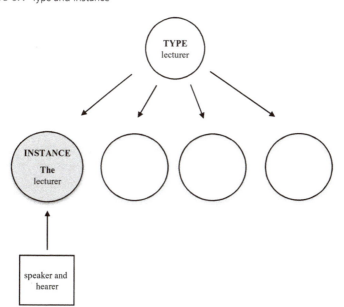

The notion of a type demonstrates how having umbrella terms for a large range of entities is practical and useful. Imagine how difficult it would be if for every lecturer we knew there was a different noun that we had to remember and use when we communicate. Lexical nouns and verbs are therefore important in that they have a classificatory function, allowing us to group things according to generally shared characteristics and use one term to refer to a larger set. It is also, of course, cognitively economical. When we require greater specificity we can identify instances through grounding strategies.

Earlier in this chapter, we identified how the verb 'mark' becomes grounded in the utterance 'The lecturer marked every assignment' through the use of the bound morpheme –ed. Given our discussion of the difference between a type and an instance, we can also explain how **clausal grounding** works to signal a particular instance; in this case it is a particular instance of an event (the marking of the assignments that has taken place in the past) that is made accessible to the hearer of the utterance since the temporal parameters of the event are now realized. Again, in this example, the ground functions as a reference point providing a contextual time frame within which the use of the past tense is understood: that is, the event took place before the time in which the speaker and hearer are now communicating (see Section 6.3 for more on clausal grounding).

Activity 6.2: Grounding in *Dracula*

Look at Text 6A. This is an extract from towards the beginning of the novel *Dracula*, written by Bram Stoker. In this extract the narrator, Jonathan Harker, uses a journal entry to recount a coach journey to Dracula's castle.

Text 6A

When we started, the crowd round the inn door, which had by this time had swelled to a considerable size, all made the sign of the cross and pointed two fingers towards me. With some difficulty I got a fellow-passenger to tell me what they meant; he would not answer at first, but on learning that I was English, he explained that it was a charm or guard against the evil eye.

(Stoker [1897] 2011: 9–10)

Identify all the examples of grounding that you can see and explain how these operate in the context of the narrative.

6.1.3 Instantiation

The process by which types become instances is known as **instantiation**. In Figure 6.1 we saw how grounding results in a particular instance of a thing or process type being profiled. Figure 6.1 is also useful in showing us that

- a type may have many possible instances;
- in seeing an instance we can acknowledge that there may be other instances of that type; and
- we can abstract backwards from any instance to see that there is an underlying type that presents a generalized way of classifying things.

It is important to remember that instantiation is a mental process and that instances can also be fictive or virtual as well as actual ones. Indeed, cognitive grammar acknowledges the fact that when we use language we often speculate, imagine or refer to as yet unrealized events – for example, when we talk about dreams, ambitions, future plans or hypothetical situations.

For example, look at Text 6B, an extract from a guide to buying a second-hand caravan.

Text 6B

Thinking of buying a second-hand caravan?
Your easy guide towards choosing a second-hand caravan

- **Choosing and buying a second-hand caravan**
- **Types of second-hand caravan available**
- **How to buy**
- **What to avoid**

> https://www.caravanclub.co.uk/media/22440/thinking
> %20of%20buying%20a%20second_hand%20caravan.pdf

The caravan referred to in this advertisement is not real but is imagined as part of a scenario in which the addressee wants to buy a caravan. Although the guide acknowledges and expects that a reader will be interested in buying an actual caravan, the referent at this point still only has a virtual existence since it is as yet unrealized outside of the hypothetical situation that the opening question establishes.

Now imagine two friends talking a little later about this guide.

A: I was thinking of buying a caravan so I read their really helpful guide.
B: Was it of any use?
A: Yes, I went and bought one right afterwards.

Here, 'a caravan' in line 1 still profiles a referent that has virtual existence. In line 3, however, the speaker B's use of the pronoun 'one' now profiles a specific, actual instance of a caravan. We have now moved beyond a hypothetical space into a real one: an actual caravan has been bought.

6.2 Nominal grounding strategies

6.2.1 Properties of nominal grounding elements

Here are four more examples of nominal grounding:

- This cold beer.
- I drank beer.
- I drank Heineken.
- I took Bob's beer.

The first example is similar to those we have previously looked at in this chapter. In this example, the demonstrative 'This' acts as a grounding element that profiles an instance of the type 'beer'. Since the grounding element singles out its referent explicitly, we can label this an **overt grounding element**. The other overt grounding elements, functioning grammatically as determiners, are shown in Table 6.1.

In the other examples, grounding occurs in different ways. The second contains an example of **covert grounding**. This type of grounding is fairly common when indeterminacy is foregrounded with plural count and mass nouns. For example in the utterances 'I met up with friends' and 'We went for coffee', there is no specificity in terms of how many friends were met or how much coffee was drunk. This grounding strategy is known as a **zero-form**, usually shown as Ø. One of the typical effects of its use is that attention is diverted to the conceptual content of the referent itself. In our two examples, the emphasis is placed on the social occasion that is associated with meeting up with friends and drinking coffee.

In 'I drank Heineken', the use of the proper noun 'Heineken' is an example of **intrinsic grounding**. Here, the uniqueness of the brand name means that no further grounding is required. In the final example, the intrinsically

Table 6.1 Overt grounding elements

Overt grounding element	Examples	Notes
Articles	*the, a*	*The* is a definite article; *a* is an indefinite article
Demonstratives	*this, that, these, those*	*This* and *that* ground singular nouns; *these* and *those* ground plural nouns; *this* and *these* are proximal demonstratives; *that* and *those* are distal demonstratives
Quantifiers	*all, most, some, no, every, each, any*	Grounding quantifiers generally profile a virtual referent

grounded possessive form 'Bob's' acts as a point of access to the noun 'beer'; the profiled instance is understood initially in relation to Bob as possessor rather than to the ground itself. Since the grounding occurs through another entity, this is known as **indirect grounding**.

There is one final point that is worth mentioning about nominal grounding at this stage. If you look closely at the four examples we have just discussed, you will see that the grounding element always occurs at the head of the nominal. We would not, for example, normally say 'cold this beer'. The principle of iconicity in cognitive grammar helps to explain this in so far as a grounding element will always provide less information about the noun than other nominal elements. In our example, the adjective 'cold' clearly gives us more information about the noun 'beer' and so occupies a more proximal position. In contrast, the grounding element 'This' merely has the function of diverting attention towards a particular instance of 'beer' so that (hopefully) the speaker and hearer focus on the same entity; it tells us nothing itself about the characteristics, taste or temperature of the beer.

It is therefore useful to think of this relationship in terms of a nominal which consists of a series of layers. The grounding element is viewed as the outer layer of the nominal, with the head noun as the core. Between these two, other layers in the form of modifying adjectives, adverbs or even other nouns are positioned in degrees of proximity to the head noun. So, for example, it would be possible to add the following additional layers to our initial nominal 'This cold beer':

- This nice smooth cold beer.

Notice in this example, the order of layering in terms of syntax reflects the relative conceptual proximity of the adjectives to the noun; in other words, being 'cold' is presented and foregrounded as being a stronger quality of the beer than its texture or overall aesthetic appeal.

Activity 6.3: Nominal grounding in non-fiction

Read Text 6C. This is an extract from 'The Good Ferry', an essay by the Canadian writer Kate Pullinger. Pullinger is writing about her experiences visiting a prison in Leicestershire where she worked with the inmates on developing their writing.

Text 6C

The prison is a couple of miles out in the country. When the weather was fine I'd cycle up the hill on the back lane, through the little hamlets with their cottages covered in rambling roses. On Gallow Field Road, HMP Gartree sits like a dark walled-in council estate that's been exiled from the town. To get inside I passed through an iron door onto a small room where I was checked over by security men on the other side of the glass. Once I was given my keys, I was allowed through another iron door, and then a whole series of locked and barred gates. Inside I'd find the men, the prisoners, and those other men, the officers, and it was like passing into another world, an elaborately hierarchical, coded, masculine world where things looked normal but once I scratched the surface, or looked again, I would discover that no, this was not a world I recognised, this was an echo world, a netherworld, to which I'd been given privileged, temporary access.

(Pullinger 1998: 109)

Identify the different types of nominal grounding that Pullinger uses and comment on their function and effect.

6.2.2 Definite reference

As we have previously discussed, the use of the definite article as a grounding element profiles a unique referent and instance of an entity. Demonstratives, however, single out rather different kinds of instances. This is related to the distinction that we made in Table 6.1 between **distal** and **proximal demonstratives**. Look at the four examples below, each of which uses a different demonstrative.

Figure 6.2 Proximal and distal regions

- This balloon
- That balloon
- These balloons
- Those balloons

In the first and third examples, the singular ('This') and plural ('These') proximal demonstratives encode *closeness* between the speaker and the referent; in the second and fourth examples, the singular ('That') and plural ('Those') distal demonstratives encode a *distance* between speaker and referent. This relationship can be shown in Figure 6.2 which demonstrates conceptually how we can show the difference between types of demonstratives using the analogy of proximal and distal spatial regions in relation to the speaker.

Interestingly, the relationship encoded by demonstratives isn't necessarily or exclusively that of *spatial* proximity or distance. Read Text 6D, an extract from Act 2, Scene 1 of Shakespeare's *Richard II*. In these lines, John of Gaunt comments on what he perceives as the sorry state of England under the rule of King Richard.

Text 6D

This royal throne of kings, this sceptred isle,
This earth of majesty, this seat of Mars,
This other Eden, demi-paradise,

This fortress built by Nature for herself
Against infection and the hand of war,
This happy breed of men, this little world,
This precious stone set in the silver sea,
Which serves it in the office of a wall
Or as a moat defensive to a house,
Against the envy of less happier lands,
This blessed plot, this earth, this realm, this England.

(*R2* 2.1.40–50)

In these lines, John of Gaunt is clearly positioning himself as physically close to England (he is speaking at the time in the country) but there are also other senses of closeness here which the extensive use of the proximal demonstrative as a grounding element seems to play out. For example, his lines hint at a temporal closeness (he is speaking about an immediate time frame), an emotional closeness (he is speaking about something which matters to him), and a functional closeness (he is speaking about an issue which has a degree of importance attached to it since he is warning about the consequences of Richard's kingship). All of these different senses foreground the various concerns held by John of Gaunt as being conceptually very close.

6.2.3 Indefinite reference

Whereas definite grounding articles single out a unique referent and instance of an entity, the use of the indefinite grounding elements operate to single out an instance from a larger **set**.

A set can be thought of as containing a number of elements that together form a larger mass. For example, there is a set of dogs from which we might select one particular instance as in the following:

- I saw a dog in the park.

In this example, the indefinite article 'a' singles out one element of the set and at the same time points to the fact that other elements were available for selection but were excluded; in this case, the excluded elements (every other dog that exists) amount to quite a considerable number.

While exclusion applies to indefinite determiners, inclusion can be said to be a property of definite reference. Since the use of definite reference draws attention to a unique instance of the referent, there are no excluded elements. The use of the definite article profiles the referent as one of a kind; compare the previous example with the one below where 'the dog' is a particular dog, either because it is known to the speaker and hearer and has been previously mentioned in the discourse or perhaps, more simply, because it is the only dog in the park at that time.

- I saw the dog in the park.

The difference in articles can also explain why the indefinite article does not combine with the superlative form of an adjective whereas the definite article does. Look at the examples below, only the second example is possible in English.

- He was a happiest child.
- He was the happiest child.

Whereas in a set of children, there can only be one 'happiest' one, if we take any other child from the set there may be predictably any number of happier individuals. This is why nominals containing a comparative adjective usually are grounded by an indefinite article as the first of the examples below, unless there are only two elements in the set as in the second example.

- He was a happier child.
- He was the happier child.

Activity 6.4: Reference in 'Meeting at night'

Read Text 6E, 'Meeting at Night', a poem by the Victorian poet Robert Browning.

Text 6E

I

The grey sea and the long black land;
And the yellow half-moon large and low;
And the startled little waves that leap
In fiery ringlets from their sleep,
As I gain the cove with pushing prow,
And quench its speed i' the slushy sand.

II

Then a mile of warm sea-scented beach;
Three fields to cross till a farm appears;
A tap at the pane, the quick sharp scratch
And blue spurt of a lighted match,

And a voice less loud, thro' its joys and fears,
Than the two hearts beating each to each!

(Browning [1849] 1989: 215)

What do you notice about the use of definite and indefinite reference?

6.3 Clausal grounding strategies

6.3.1 The difference between nominal and clausal grounding

As we have seen so far in this chapter, nominal grounding elements are used to evoke a particular instance of a type so as to allow both speaker and hearer mental access to a referent that is identifiable within the ground.

In contrast, clausal grounding strategies reflect the fact that verbs are representations of events or processes. So, whereas nominal grounding acts as a kind of selection strategy to identify an instance of a type, clausal grounding relates events to our conception of knowledge in the world; in other words, how does the event being profiled fit into what we currently know and our own sense of reality? In the remainder of this chapter, we will look at two clausal grounding strategies: tense and modality.

6.3.2 Reality

We will begin, however, by exploring the important concept of reality in more detail. Imagine the following utterances spoken by one friend to another about the 100-metres men's athletics final at the 2017 World Championships (which had just taken place at the time of writing this book).

- The 100-metres is one of the showcase events at the Championships.
- Usain Bolt won the last 100-metres World Championships gold medal in Beijing 2015.
- The 100-metres final will be on Saturday evening.
- Usain Bolt may get beaten this time around.

In each of these instances, the speaker is using current knowledge of the world as a benchmark to assess the truth of the utterances. In the first example, the speaker draws on established and generally accepted knowledge about the status of the 100-metres final that is true at the time of speaking. In the second, the speaker again draws on established knowledge, here specifically relaying a fact that occurred in the past. In the third, the speaker refers to an event that is expected to happen, while in the fourth example, there is speculation about the possibility of an event.

We can say that each of the utterances fits into a **model of reality**, shown in Figure 6.3.

In this model, the conceptualizer relays events with respect to an assessment of reality. Since reality is bound up with the motion of time, the conceptualizer perceives reality in relation to the past, present and future alongside a sense of **evolutionary momentum**. As the conceptualizer moves through time, she also perceives knowledge as belonging to a different aspect or concept of reality. These can be summarized as follows:

- **conceived reality**: consisting of events that we know about and are established as having happened in the past;

- **immediate reality**: consisting of events that we are aware of at the present moment in time;

- **projected reality**: consisting of events that we can be reasonably sure of occurring based on our existing knowledge;

- **potential reality**: consisting of events that could possibly happen;

- **irreality**: consisting of events that either have not happened or of which we have no knowledge whatsoever.

Figure 6.3 Model of reality (based on Langacker 1991a)

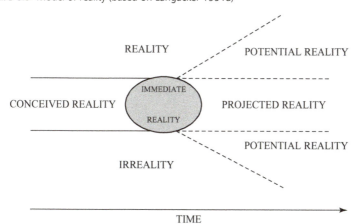

We can now relate the utterances about the athletics World Championships into the model of reality.

The first example is established knowledge and the speaker is therefore communicating that the situation is conceived reality. In this instance the use of the present tense functions to present the event as a kind of general truth and so grounds the situation being described as conceived reality. In the second, the speaker also presents the situation as conceived reality, this time through the use of the past tense. In the third, however, the speaker is referring to an event that has yet to take place. In this instance, given that the speaker can be reasonably sure that the final will take place on Saturday (based on previous knowledge and the fact that the men's 100-metres final has been scheduled for the Saturday evening), the situation forms part of projected reality and is grounded as such through the use of the future-tense form 'will be'. Finally, in the fourth example, the speaker assesses the possibility of Usain Bolt getting beaten. Here the use of the modal auxiliary verb 'may' grounds the situation in potential reality.

6.3.3 Tense

As we have seen in the previous section, tense is important in terms of grounding in so far as it shows how an event exists in time relative to the speaker's perspective or stance. In our World Championships examples, we saw how the speaker was positioning herself and a mental representation of the event being discussed in relation to time by looking backwards or forwards, in each case grounding the situation being described within one kind of reality. Tense is therefore defined as the grammatical configuration of the mental concept of time.

As we discussed earlier in this chapter, in cognitive grammar the context involving a speech event, its participants and its time and place is known as the ground. Tense is a way of showing how different aspects of time can be perceived as relative to the ground and are related to the concepts of **speech time** and **event time**. For example, imagine the following exchange:

You: What are you doing?
Your friend: I am reading a book.

The use of the present progressive tense shows that the event being described is taking place at the moment of speaking. In other words, the moment of speaking (speech time) is equivalent to the time of the event (event time).

Now imagine that your friend hands you the book and you start reading it. It is the novel *Miss Peregrine's Home for Peculiar Children*, by Ransom

Riggs. You start reading a few pages into Chapter 2 where the narrator recounts telling the police about what he witnessed on the night his grandfather was killed. This section is reprinted as Text 6F. Of course, in this instance a different kind of interaction, this time between you and a narrator (and ultimately an author) is taking place.

Text 6F

Even my best and only friend Ricky didn't believe me, and he'd been there. He swore up and down that he hadn't seen any creature in the woods that night – even though I'd shined my flashlight right at it – which is just what he told the cops. He heard barking, though. We both had. So it wasn't a huge surprise when the police concluded that a pack of feral wolves had killed my grandfather. Apparently they'd been spotted somewhere else and had taken bites out of a woman who'd been walking in the Century Woods the week before.

Riggs (2011: 42)

In this extract Jacob uses the past tense 'didn't believe', which directs the reader to a previous narrative event (Ricky saying that he doesn't believe him). As the narrator of the novel, Jacob, speaks to us as we read (even if he is a fictional entity), the past tense reflects this looking back from the vantage point of the current ground. In this instance event time is clearly before speech time. As we read, another pattern emerges that highlights a different time frame. The use of the past tense 'he'd been there' shifts the narrative action to a time frame even further back (Ricky and Jacob in the woods). Here, event time is markedly before speech time; indeed, the speaker looks back not from the current ground but from the initial past event (where Ricky says that he doesn't believe him). In this instance, Jacob, as narrator, uses the past event of talking to his friend Ricky as a reference point (look back at Chapter 4 for a definition and discussion of reference points in cognitive grammar) for accessing this different time frame. In fact as we read through the remainder of this extract we can see more instances where Jacob shifts his vantage point to a past event that acts as a reference point to allow access to narrative events, for example, through the past tense clauses 'he swore up and down' and 'he told the cops'.

Finally, imagine that having put the book down, your friend now says to you 'I'll finish this book tomorrow'. In this instance, this utterance directs you to think of an event that will exist after speech time rather than before it. Taken together, these examples show a speaker can use tense to project backwards or forwards in order to locate a hearer within the time frame of an event.

6.4 Modality

6.4.1 A definition of modality

In Section 6.3.2 we discussed how modal verbs ground situations in potential reality. In this section, we will explore modality in more detail, beginning with a definition of modality in cognitive grammar terms.

Look at Text 6G, which contains further examples of modality (all in italics).

Text 6G

Vehicle tax and insurance rules

All vehicles on the road, apart from those exempt from vehicle tax because they are designed for use by disabled people or have zero CO_2 emissions, for example, *must* be both taxed and insured

Fail to do this, and you *will* face penalties such as an automatic fine of £80, plus any tax arrears

You *could* even be prosecuted in court for driving without insurance

But if you have a car or van that you do not use and is kept off the public roads, you *can* avoid vehicle tax and the need for insurance by registering the vehicle as off the road.

To do this, you *must* file a SORN.

http://www.moneysupermarket.com/car-insurance/blog/everything-you-need-to-know-about-the-statutory-off-road-notification-sorn/

In each of these examples, the modal auxiliary verb carries some kind of energy or force that leads to an event occurring. For example, 'must' has an inherent power that compels a car owner to tax their vehicle. We should note that in this instance, the power is more psychological and social than physical (and is of course supported by the institutional force of the law). In cognitive grammar, however, it is important to remember that modal verbs are understood in terms of taking their meaning from our concepts of force and movement in the physical world. We will return to this point in Section 6.4.3.

We can look at the other modal verbs in this text to demonstrate how modality relates to potential reality. For example, 'will' is a strong marker of potential in that it shows a high level of commitment towards an event occurring; in this case, we could argue it borders on projected reality. In contrast, 'could' presents a lower degree of certainty, as does 'can'. This brief discussion shows that there are different types of modality with both subtle and not-so-subtle differences in form and meaning. At this stage, however, we can sketch out a beginning definition of modality as the phenomenon that shows a speaker's attitude towards the potentiality of an event. Because modality focuses on potential reality, it is future oriented. And, because modal forms derive from our understanding of force, we can say they are force-dynamic (see Section 6.4.3).

6.4.2 Types of modality

So far, we have looked at modality and its relationship to the notions of reality and potentiality in broad terms. We can, however, categorize different types of modality that provide more nuanced explanations of how modal constructions work.

Deontic modality: concerned with aspects of obligation and permission
Epistemic modality: concerned with degrees of certainty and possibility
Boulomaic modality: concerned with aspects of desire
Dynamic modality: concerned with aspects of ability

The examples of modality we have seen so far have all been expressed using modal auxiliary verbs but modal constructions can also take other forms, for example:

- modal clauses, for example, 'there is every chance that …', 'It's got to be the case that …';
- modal adjectives, for example, 'possible', 'probable';
- modal adverbs, for example, 'perhaps', 'certainly';
- modal lexical verbs, for example, 'like', 'want';
- modal tags (expressions at the end of utterances), for example, 'I guess', 'imho' (in my humble opinion).

Activity 6.5: Types and forms of modality

Identify the type and form of each of the following examples of modality.

1 I *want* to buy a car.
2 Alan *must* be home by now.
3 You *must* close the door.
4 It's *possible* to lose everything.
5 They are *probably* late.

6 *Can* you play the guitar?

7 My friend *may* be visiting me this evening.

8 Liverpool *will* win the league this year.

9 You *should* leave now.

10 *I am sure that* he borrowed my book.

A key difference between deontic and epistemic modal forms is that deontic modals function to bring about an occurrence. In example 3, the speaker aims to make the hearer close the door; the use of the modal 'must' will usually carry a potency that brings to effect the closing of the door. Deontic modal forms are therefore understood as bringing about the grounding process. A construction like an imperative form or clause operates in a similar way. For example, the utterance 'Close the door' has no internal grounding element but is understood as conveying the same meaning as 'You must close the door' and is clearly outside of conceived reality when spoken (since the closing of door has not yet happened).

Epistemic forms, however, are concerned with certainty and possibility and are used to assess the relative status of the occurrence in relation to the speaker's notion of conceived reality (for past and current events) and projected or potential reality (for future events). In this way, the force inherent in the modal form functions to convince the speaker (or not) of the likelihood of an event's occurrence. This can be seen in example 2, where 'must' does not influence whether or when Alan will get home but instead acts to position the event within the speaker's notion of conceived reality; in example 7, where 'may' places the occurrence in potential reality; and in example 8, where 'will' places the occurrence in projected reality.

6.4.3 Force dynamics

The concept of force is ubiquitous. You can think of how we experience force in a physical sense in a number of different everyday experiences, for example, when we bump into something, pick an object up and throw it or when we are pushed back by a strong wind. Force usually involves some kind of source of imposition, someone or something that is responsible for initiating an action. It is also largely interactive in that the force emanates from a source but also affects another entity. For example, you can pick up a ball and apply a force to it that causes it to leave your hand and travel some distance to a new resting point. In this case, you are the source of energy and the ball is affected by the force in so far as it is moved. We can also experience force in a psychological or social sense. For example, a manager in a company might say to an employee 'You must complete that work today'. In this case, the force that emanates from the source (the manager) works on the employee in a psychological sense and is framed by an explicit social relationship (the fact that the employer holds institutional power).

As we saw in Section 6.4.1, in cognitive grammar modal verbs can be understood as inherently containing some degree of energy, force or potency. In Section 6.4.2 we discussed how for deontic modals, this potency has an external consequence in that it serves to effect the grounding process while for epistemic modals, the potency is internal and assesses the likelihood of the speaker accepting an event's occurrence.

Modal forms can also be understood in image-schematic terms. As we saw in Chapter 2, in cognitive linguistics more generally, an image schema is a basic template that arises naturally from the various bodily and spatial interactions we have in our physical environments. For example, we develop a basic FORCE schema from our experiences of force and counterforce in the physical world and this provides a structure for mental and social operations such as giving orders, allowing permission and presenting an opinion.

Let's return to our discussion of the inherent difference between deontic and epistemic modals in Section 6.4.2 as a way of exemplifying image schemas and force.

1 You *must* close the door (deontic form of must).

2 Alan *must* be home by now (epistemic form of must).

In both cases, the force inherent in 'must' is based on a COMPULSION schema, shown in Figure 6.4, where one entity exerts a force on another entity. The other entity offers a weaker counterforce (shown by the dotted line) and is unable to offer resistance.

Figures 6.5 and 6.6 show how the difference in deontic and epistemic modality relates to **force dynamics**. In Figure 6.5, the speaker is the source of energy and imposes a force through some degree of social authority or power on an agent who by consequence has less power and therefore offers a weaker counterforce. The modal form operates to make the event (the closing of the door) happen.

In Figure 6.6, however, the epistemic status of the event (Alan's being at home) is foregrounded through the use of 'must'. In this example, the modal verb shows that there is a high degree of certainty in the reality status of the utterance. The force behind the utterance is internal to the speaker and

Figure 6.4 COMPULSION schema

Figure 6.5 Force dynamics of deontic modality in 'you must close the door'

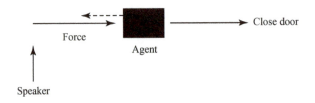

Figure 6.6 Force dynamics of epistemic modality in 'Alan must be at home'

Figure 6.7 Continua of epistemic assessment and deontic necessity: weak to strong

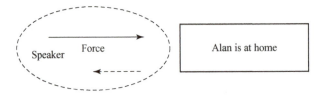

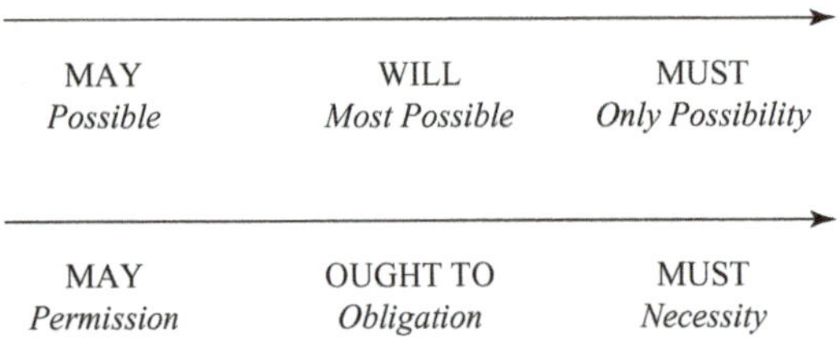

is stronger than any opposing counterforce of doubt or uncertainty that the speaker may be feeling. The epistemic modal form shows that, at the moment of speaking, knowledge available to the speaker leads him to believe that the possibility of what is said being right is very strong. The force thus acts on the speaker's assessment of the proposition rather than any additional entity.

6.4.4 Gradience

The example of epistemic modality that we have just looked at demonstrates that **gradience** is another key feature of modality. Just as forces have degrees of power and intensity, modality offers a way of conceptualizing different degrees of possibility and certainty, desire, capability and necessity. Figure 6.7 shows a continua of epistemic and deontic modal auxiliary verbs.

Activity 6.6: Degrees of modality

The foregrounding of a particular degree of modality in texts can yield strong interpretative effects. Look at Text 6H, an extract from 'In the Dark', a short supernatural story by E. Nesbit.

Text 6H

> It may have been a form of madness. Or it may be that he really was what is called haunted. Or it may – though I don't pretend to understand how – have been the development, through intense suffering, of a sixth sense in a very nervous, highly-strung nature.
>
> (Nesbit [1893] 2016: 111)

What might the function and effect of the modal pattern established be?

6.5 Extended example analysis: *The Girl on the Train*

The following section draws together all the ideas and concepts covered in this chapter in an example analysis of Text 6I, an extract from Paula Hawkins' novel *The Girl on the Train*. In this extract, the narrator, Rachel, is an alcoholic who has witnessed a crucial event in the disappearance of another woman, Megan. Her alcoholism has, however, left her incapable of remembering exactly what she saw or was doing on the night that Megan went missing. At this point in the novel, she is wondering what her next step might be: to try to find another traveller she met that evening or to contact Scott, Megan's husband. Rachel had previously been reported to the police for allegedly harassing her ex-husband Tom and his wife, Anna, who live in the same street as Megan.

Text 6I

> I spent yesterday evening sitting on the sofa in jogging bottoms and a T-shirt, making lists of things to do, possible strategies. For example, I could hang around Witney station at rush hour, wait until I see the red-haired man from Saturday night again. I could invite him for a drink and see where it leads, whether he saw anything, what he knows about the night. The danger is that I might see Anna or Tom, they would report me and I would get into trouble (more trouble) with the police. The other danger is that I

might make myself more vulnerable. I still have the trace of an argument in my head – I may have the physical evidence of it on my scalp and lip. What if this is the man who hurt me? The fact that he smiled and waved doesn't mean anything, he could be a psychopath for all I know. But I can't see him as a psychopath. I can't explain it, but I warm to him.

I could contact Scott again. But I need to give him a reason to talk to me, and I'm worried that whatever I say will make me look like a mad woman. He might even think I had something to do with Megan's disappearance, he could report me to the police. I could end up in real trouble.

I could try hypnosis. I'm pretty sure it won't help me remember anything, but I'm curious about it anyway. It can't hurt can it?

(Hawkins 2015: 135–6)

Rachel is one of three narrators in the novel (the others are Anna and Megan) and so the entire narrative events are framed from the point of view of one of these characters and filtered through a specific fictional consciousness. Rachel is an alcoholic and Hawkins explores the effects of her abuse on her ability to recollect events throughout the novel. This extract is therefore representative of a wider concern of showing the presentation of a particular mind. Throughout the novel, Rachel construes situations and events in certain ways that is representative of her alcoholism. She quite clearly frames herself (in this extract and throughout the remainder of the novel) as a kind of pseudo-detective, attempting to solve both the case of Megan's disappearance and her own role in it. In fact throughout the novel, Rachel engages constantly in this type of search for the truth as she struggles to cope with her own alcoholism, which has placed severe constraints on her ability to recall past events. In this extract, Rachel emphasizes this role through the nouns that she uses as she presents her thoughts – for example 'strategies' and 'evidence' – which indicate an attempt to employ some kind of deliberate methodology. The extract begins in the past tense, a normative narrative strategy that is also the pattern in the novel, with the first event (Rachel's recount of 'yesterday') grounded in conceived reality. Following this, however, the narrative becomes highly modalized, which in turn reveals a mind and voice that is represented as uncertain in its ability to accurately recount previous events.

The dominant pattern that appears is epistemic modality, largely through the use of modal auxiliary verbs such as 'may' and 'might' that present Rachel's assessment of the situations that she narrates as relatively weak. Equally, the dynamic modal auxiliary verb 'could' is here used in a more or less epistemic sense to convey a further aspect of Rachel's uncertainty. Her use of perception modality, such as the lexical verbs 'see', 'look', and modal clauses 'I'm worried that' and 'I'm pretty sure it won't', demonstrates how the relative status of events both past and anticipated are presented to emphasize a limited epistemic assessment of events. Where stronger modal forms are used – for example, in 'they would report me and I would get into trouble' – they convey negative consequences for Rachel; her ability to reflect with any certainty on future events is, it appears, restricted to a straightforward understanding of the consequence of her behaviour based on her previous experiences. Even when Rachel uses categorical (non-modal) statements – for example, in 'the fact that he smiled and waved doesn't mean anything' – the negated syntax of the main clause, 'doesn't mean', serves to potentially deny the reliability or meaning of any assumption that Rachel makes about her ability to read and assess the situation.

In terms of nominal grounding, the singular certainty that Rachel holds (the recount of sitting at home on the previous evening) is echoed in the overt grounding strategy and the use of the definite article in 'the sofa'. Her familiarity and proximity to that particular physical space is reflected in the way she singles out the referent in this instance. Less relevant details such as the clothes she is wearing are revealed through indefinite reference, 'a t-shirt', or through the use of zero-form grounding, 'jogging bottoms'; the elliptical form in this latter example also reflects the conversational register of Rachel's narrative.

Further nominalization across the extract includes the intrinsically grounded proper nouns 'Witney station', 'Anna' and 'Tom' – all of which are fairly stable entities in Rachel's consciousness and the definite reference, 'the red-haired man'. Interestingly, the man (referenced before in the novel and therefore available for mental access through the use of a definite determiner) remains definite and memorable enough for Rachel to reference him through the use of the premodifying compound adjective 'red-haired', but not so memorable as to be able to refer to him by name. Generally, nominal grounding in the extract appears to move between definiteness – 'the night' – and indefiniteness –'a drink'. This mirrors Rachel's own partial recollection of key events and the mismatch between her ability to recall vivid aspects, such as the colour of the man's hair and any other information that might be valuable in piecing together what happened. Indeed the extract appears to operate within the principle of iconicity, in that formal content matches conceptual content: 'an argument' is indefinite and vague and demonstrates a lack of awareness of the actual circumstances of the event, whereas the definite reference of 'the physical evidence' and the indirect grounding through the possessive determiner in 'my scalp and lip' profile creates more substantive – and concrete – reminders of the event of the night before. Indefinite reference is also used to open up access to new mental spaces that represent potentially significant plot and thematic concerns of the novel. So new ideas are introduced into the ground such as 'a psychopath' and 'a mad woman' although these are understood within previously discussed and available detail, the definite reference of 'the police' and the indirectly grounded 'Megan's disappearance'.

Overall then, we could argue that the grounding in this extract functions as a way of representing Rachel's thinking and her attempts to remember previous events and rationalize her future decisions. New details and thoughts are activated and combine with memories that are vague and which Rachel finds difficult to adequately express. Her own uncertainty towards the epistemic assessment of the propositions she narrates is marked through the extensive use of epistemic and perception modalities that signal a disorientated, questioning and, ultimately for the reader, an unreliable fictional consciousness and mind. This particular degree of 'modal shading' (Simpson 1993) serves to provide a stark fictional representation of a mind that is struggling with the effects of alcoholism, and in particular, with an ability to recount past events precisely and, by consequence, attach any future significance to them.

6.6 Further activities

1.
Read Text 6J, the opening lines to the first stanza of 'The Canonization' by John Donne.

Text 6J

> For God's sake hold your tongue, and let me love,
> Or chide my palsy, or my gout,
> My five gray hairs, or ruined fortune flout,
> With wealth your state, your mind with arts improve,
> Take you a course, get you a place,
> Observe his honor, or his grace,
> Or the king's real, or his stampèd face
> Contemplate, what you will, approve,
> So you will let me love.

(Donne [1633] 1994: 6)

What do you notice about the types of nominal and clausal grounding in this extract?

2.

Read Text 6K, taken from an online holiday guide to Majorca. The extract is advertising a day trip to an outdoor shopping market.

Text 6K

Inca Market & Festival Park

If you're anything of a shopaholic, you'll love this. The morning is dedicated to Majorca's largest outdoor market. It starts with a coach ride to Inca, a working town in the heart of the island. Here, you'll get ample free time to wander around the stands and shop till you drop. Think tables creaking under the weight of fresh fruit, cheeses, herbs and olives. Trestle tables stacked with straw baskets, African masks and budget clothes. And racks and racks of the leather bags, sandals and shoes that Inca is famous for. Put simply, if it's Majorcan you can pretty much bet you'll find it here. You'll then travel to Majorca's only outlet centre – Festival Park. You'll have just over an hour to browse the stores, that include well-known brands like Levi's, Nike and Lacoste. We'll even give you an exclusive book of discount vouchers that you can use in all the shops. This is shopping at its best.

http://www.thomson.co.uk/destinations/attraction/
Alcudia/Inca-Market-&-Festival-Park-991462

1 What do you notice about the use of modality in this extract?

2 Identify and discuss any patterns you can see as well as any particular modal expressions that you feel are interesting.

3 How does the text use modality in relation to non-modal (categorical) expressions?

3.

Find examples of extracts from both literary and non-literary texts that contain dominant and/or interesting patterns of modality. How can you relate the use of modal forms to narrative point of view, genre, purpose and implied readership?

6.7 Further reading

Chapter 9 of Langacker (2008) offers an overview of instantiation, grounding and grounding strategies. Grounding is also covered in Taylor (2002: 246–65) and Chapter 5 of Radden and Dirven (2007). The concepts of type and instance are also covered in more detail in Chapter 2 of Langacker (1991).

Definiteness is covered in Epstein (2001). The model of reality discussed in this chapter is taken from Langacker (1991) and is also discussed in Langacker (2008: 300–9). The notion of force dynamics comes from Talmy (1988) and is also discussed extensively in Sweetser (1990). Johnson (1987) explores modality in relation to image schemas. Comprehensive cognitive linguistic overviews of modality can be found in Nuyts (2006) and Chapter 10 of Radden and Dirven (2007). Outside of cognitive linguistics, modality is covered more generally in Coates (1983) and Palmer (2001). Interesting accounts of gradience as a property of modality include Hodge and Kress (1988) and Halliday and Matthiessen (2013). Simpson (1993) introduces and discusses his 'modal grammar' in relation to point of view with reference to a range of literary texts and discussion of the various functions and effects of 'modal shading'. Gavins (2005) provides a comprehensive coverage of modality within her own development of Text World Theory (Werth 1999). Work in stylistics that addresses concepts in this chapter includes Harrison (2017a) on grounding and narrative urgency, Giovanelli (2018a) on nominal grounding and mind style in Paula Hawkins' *The Girl on the Train*, Browse (2014) on force dynamics and modality, and Tabakowska (2014) on epistemic modality and point of view. Giovanelli (2013) integrates Langacker's ideas on modality into Text World Theory, and analyses point of view in the poems of John Keats in terms of the stylistic functions and effects of different modal forms. Browse (2018) has a chapter-length treatment of grounding in relation to political discourse.

Chapter 7
Discourse

In this chapter we will explore:

- what is meant by discourse within the context of grammar;
- the scalability of the central components of cognitive grammar for the analysis of larger units of language; and
- the potential areas for future research and application.

7.1 Grammar above the sentence

As outlined in Chapter 1, this book has been structured such that as we have generally moved up the linguistic rank scale we have introduced new ideas from cognitive grammar. The early chapters introduced word meanings, the constructions of nouns and verbs and viewing arrangements in language. The latter chapters have moved on to consider how these examples of language can be contextualized – and, importantly, Chapter 5 introduced the idea of the clause: a unit of language that is headed by a verb process that plays a key role in the communication of experience. In other words, we have been dealing with increasingly larger units of language – or, in cognitive grammar terms, we have been moving from the local to the global organization of language.

While this has helped structure the introduction of these key cognitive grammar ideas, we have, at the same time, also presented examples of, and analyses using, cognitive grammar in relation to constructions of language that are bigger than a clause: to posters, to short extracts and paragraphs from stories, to longer passages from texts and to poems in their entirety and so on. This is because, in order to carry out a comprehensive and successful stylistic analysis, it is helpful – and, arguably, necessary – to be able to talk about how language patterns work at all levels of the text: the micro- (e.g. individual word choices), the meso- (e.g. patterns across sentences) and the macro-levels (e.g. the text in its entirety; the implications of context, etc.) of language. Such applications have enabled us to treat central ideas from cognitive grammar as scalable tools: as frameworks that work across all levels of linguistic construction.

Using cognitive grammar in this way departs from the original research into the theory, which instead focused on constructions of language up to the level of the clause – despite identifying the potential for cognitive grammar to be scalable for larger usage events. Consequently, using cognitive grammar in this way is a new area of research, and one which has only just begun to be explored.

This last point is important to remember as you read through this chapter. In other words, do think critically about the ideas presented here. While we have striven to present accessible and convincing discourse analyses using cognitive grammar across this book, many of these ideas would certainly benefit from further road-testing. There is much more work to be carried out regarding testing cognitive grammar's scalability, and this means that there are many exciting avenues of research ahead.

7.2 The current discourse space: Spoken discourse

When 'discourse' is broached in original accounts of cognitive grammar, it is discussed in relation to speech events: spoken discourse. It is argued that, when we speak, we produce a usage event. This is defined as an instance of language use that comprises both phonetic parts (i.e. the exact way we vocalize the expression), and wider contextual information speakers/listeners need in order to understand the expression. Similarly, we can differentiate between linguistic meaning (semantics) and the more holistic meaning which also comprises extralinguistic resources (pragmatics).

A usage event requires a speaker/hearer to conceptualize both the ground and the current discourse space (CDS). An expression never takes place in a vacuum; its interpretation is always supported by a specific discourse context. As noted in Chapter 6, the ground of a usage event is made up of particular pieces of information: the speaker and hearer, what is being said (their interaction) and when and where the speech event takes place. On the other hand, the **CDS** is a mental space that carries information about the wider context of the interaction. In other words, it is a conceptual model that we build and adapt in order to interpret ongoing discourse events. This can be represented as in Figure 7.1.

Figure 7.1 The current discourse space. Diagram after Langacker (2001: 145)

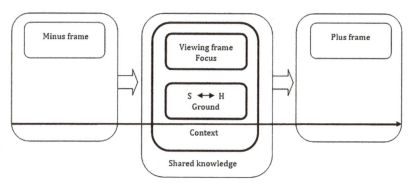

The **viewing frame** of the CDS is described as the visual field of the speaker and hearer (N.B. This label is arguably somewhat misleading, as of course we are able to have conversations about things and circumstances we are not immediately seeing or experiencing), whereas the **focus** is the particular aspect of the visual field the interlocutors are paying attention to at any given moment. An ongoing collaborative conversation would also comprise earlier usage events (minus frames) and anticipated utterances (plus frames), which may or may not be referenced explicitly in the current interaction, but which nevertheless influence the conversation and impact on the direction of the exchange in some way. The plus frames of discourse, in particular, relate to our expectations about what will appear next in the interaction. Such discourse expectations occur at all levels of language: we would assume, for example, that a verb profile would have an inflection; that 'therefore' would be followed by an explanation; 'because' followed by a reason, and so on.

Since we are initially thinking about these ideas in relation to spoken discourse, it might be helpful to first think about how this works in fictional dialogue. Let us revisit Text 7A, the exchange between Jack and Algernon used in Chapter 5, as an example:

Text 7A

Jack: How can you sit there, calmly eating muffins when we are in this horrible trouble, I can't make out. You seem to me to be perfectly heartless.

Algernon: Well, I can't eat muffins in an agitated manner. The butter would probably get on my cuffs. One should always eat muffins quite calmly. It is the only way to eat them.

Jack: I say it's perfectly heartless you're eating muffins at all, under the circumstances.

Algernon: When I am in trouble, eating is the only thing that consoles me.
Indeed, when I am in really great trouble, as any one who knows me
intimately will tell you, I refuse everything except food and drink. At the
present moment I am eating muffins because I am unhappy. Besides,
I am particularly fond of muffins. [*Rising*]
Jack: [*Rising*] Well, that is no reason why you should eat them all in that
greedy way. [*Takes muffins from Algernon.*]
Algernon: [*Offering tea-cake*] I wish you would have tea-cake instead.
I don't like tea-cake.

(Wilde [1898] 1999: 69)

A range of information is needed in order to comprehend the specific discourse context of this exchange. As the two interlocutors in this conversation, Jack and Algernon alternate between speaker/hearer roles. Those who
are familiar with the play will know that the reason for the 'horrible trouble'
is referenced in the previous exchange (minus frames) of discourse. In this
previous exchange the two other protagonists, Cecily and Gwendolen, have
discovered that Jack and Algernon are not both named 'Ernest', as they had
previously believed. As a consequence, Cecily and Gwendolen have retreated
angrily into the house, leaving Jack and Algernon in the garden. Evidently,
the entire scene of the two characters having afternoon tea in the garden constitutes the viewing frame of this particular discourse event, and the interaction is also clearly grounded in the present ('At the present moment I am
eating muffins because I am unhappy'). Further, the conversation itself is
collaborative, as both characters share the same focus of conversation (i.e.
they are discussing what they are eating): the mentions of muffins serve as a
reference point to renew this topic as the focus of the conversation in each of
the turns. In terms of the anticipated frames of discourse, first-time viewers or
readers may be unsure of what to expect next in the interaction, but may draw
on contextual knowledge about the play in order to make a guess. Contextual
information would help here: they would be aware, for example, of the genre
of the play (comedy), and perhaps guess at some romantic reconciliation
between the two pairs of protagonists.

Activity 7.1: Spoken discourse in *Big Bang Theory*

Read Text 7B, a piece of dialogue from the American sitcom *Big Bang Theory*.
In this scene, Penny, a new friend, is visiting Leonard and Sheldon's apartment to share a takeaway with them. She sits on the sofa in Sheldon's 'spot',
not knowing that he is very particular about (among other things) where he
sits.

Text 7B

Penny: Can I start?

Sheldon: Erm Penny. That's where I sit.

Penny: So sit next to me.

Sheldon: No. I sit there.

Penny: What's the difference?

Sheldon: What's the difference?

Leonard: Here we go.

Sheldon: In the winter that seat is close enough to the radiator to stay warm and yet not so close as to cause perspiration. In the summer it's directly in the path of a cross-breeze created by opening windows there and there. It faces the television at an angle which is neither direct thus discouraging conversation nor far wide as to create a parallax distortion. I could go on but I think I've made my point.

Penny: Do you want me to move?

Sheldon: Well –

Leonard: Just sit somewhere else.

Sheldon: Fine. (*Awkwardly moves around the room approaching different seats*)

Leonard: Sheldon – sit.

Sheldon: (*Sits down*) Ah.

In pairs, identify what pieces of CDS information are established in the text and consider the following questions:

1 How does the focus of the interaction alter between the conversational turns and throughout the exchange as a whole?

2 Does it seem as though all of the discourse participants have the same level of 'shared knowledge'? If not, what tensions are created?

3 In your view, does this model effectively capture both the semantic and pragmatic properties of the interaction?

7.3 The role of the reader

Of course, where the CDS structure gets complicated for stylistic analysis is when we try to apply these ideas to reading – or, as in this example of dialogue from a play, when we consider the role of an audience member. The complicating factor is that, outside of the conversation, there is an offstage viewer who plays an integral role in the comprehension of the interaction, in response to the linguistic cues selected by the author. This can be roughly represented as in Figure 7.2.

Just like the relationship between the speaker and hearer in a spoken exchange, a relationship between an audience member and playwright, or a reader and writer, is also needed in order for the exchange to take place. This relationship is similarly built upon contextual information, wider shared knowledge, knowledge about previous usage events and expectations about usage events to come, and also requires the two participants to share a viewing frame/focus. When we read a text, we are invited to conceptualize the relationship between 'S' and 'H' – the discourse participants within the fictional world – too. The CDS therefore becomes more complicated through the fact that information about these various relationships needs to be conceptualized simultaneously.

Furthermore, it can be argued that while construal (see Chapter 3) has traditionally referred to how a scene has been encoded by a linguistic producer (speaker, author, playwright, etc.), it is also a process that occurs at the reception end of linguistic events. Readers or listeners will pay greater attention to certain things, places, people, events and so forth, with which they have stronger schematic associations. Of course, the importance of the role of a reader in creating meaning can in turn impact upon how an entire text is experienced, and therefore has important implications for the analysis of texts as a whole.

Figure 7.2 The current discourse space in the context of reading

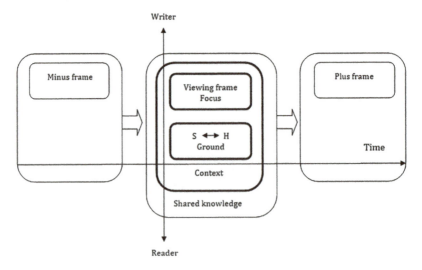

Activity 7.2: Meaning-making

This next activity draws together the ideas presented so far in this chapter to consider the important role of readers in meaning-making, and how the conceptualization of the relationships in the CDS (the representation of the characters and their context/knowledge, as well as the shared knowledge between the real-world author and reader) can be manipulated through stylistic cues to achieve particular literary effects, or a particular reading experience.

Elizabeth Is Missing (Healey 2014) is a pseudo-detective story narrated by the protagonist Maud, who has dementia. The following quotations in Text 7C are examples of her descriptions of everyday objects.

Text 7C

  a 'bread-heater, the bread browner' (Healey 2014: 82);

  b 'his neckcloth thing, not a scarf, not a cravat' (Healey 2014: 154);

  c 'a packet of lamp posts, tiny lamp posts with lead through the middle' (Healey 2014: 217).

  1 What is Maud describing in each of these quotations? How do we know this?

  2 As mentioned in Chapter 4, in cognitive grammar reference points are defined as salient parts of the landscape around which other things can be oriented. We used the example of giving someone directions, using more prominent parts of the landscape (reference points) to direct them to a less salient destination (target). The range of potential targets generated are said to form the dominion of a reference point. What reference points does Maud draw on in order to describe these targets? What is the effect of describing them in this way?

  3 Describing everyday objects like this is a stylistic trait of Maud's in the novel. How would such descriptions impact on our construction of the CDS? If such descriptions and reference point relationships are a key style feature of the novel, how would this impact on the experience of reading the novel as a whole?

7.4 Extended example analysis

So far in this chapter we have introduced the idea of how particular mental spaces – that combine to build a CDS – can be constructed, maintained and drawn upon in the comprehension of spoken discourse, specifically. But of course, we also need cognitive grammar to be able to account for larger patterns of language in written texts. For such analyses, it is helpful to return to some of the other key ideas from cognitive grammar, and draw them together for a more holistic account of style patterns in and across a text.

The Shining is a horror novel written by Stephen King and first published in 1977. The story begins with the character Jack Torrance, an aspiring author, being offered the job of caretaker during the off-season at the Overlook Hotel in the Rocky Mountains. His five-year-old son, Danny, has a psychic ability referred to as 'the shining', which allows him to see events that have happened as well as those to come. The story follows Jack's gradual descent into madness as he and his family stay at the hotel during the winter months.

This selected extract, Text 7D, is taken from the ominously titled chapter 'The Wasp's Nest'. In this scene, Danny is standing outside room 217 – a particular room in the hotel that he has been repeatedly told not to visit, but to which he feels drawn. The extract describes his worry about entering the room, and features multiple spectral voices that his psychic ability allows him to hear. The analysis below draws on a range of ideas from cognitive grammar (the construction of the CDS, grounding, construal and domains) to address how the feelings of horror and suspense are generated in this extract through the stylistic patterns that run throughout.

Text 7D

Danny was standing outside room 217 again.

The passkey was in his pocket. He was staring at the door with a kind of drugged avidity, and his upper body seemed to twitch and jiggle beneath his flannel shirt. He was humming softly and tunelessly.

[...]

What he had seen in the Presidential Sweet had gone away. And the snake had only been a fire hose that had fallen onto the rug. Yes, even the blood in the Presidential Sweet had been harmless, something old, something that had happened long before he was born or even thought of, something that was done with. Like a movie that only he could see. There was nothing, really nothing, in this hotel that could hurt him, and if he had to prove that to himself by going into this room, shouldn't he do so?

'Lou, Lou, skip to m'Lou ...'

(*Curiosity killed the cat my dear redrum, redrum my dear, satisfaction brought him back safe and sound, from toes to crown; from head to ground he was safe and sound. He knew that those things*)

(*are like scary pictures, they can't hurt you, but oh my god*)

(what big teeth you have grandma and is that a wolf in a BLUEBEARD
suit or a BLUEBEARD in a wolf suit and I'm so)

(glad you asked because curiosity killed that cat and it was the HOPE of
satisfaction that brought him)

up the hall, treading softly over the blue and twisting jungle carpet. He
had stopped by the fire extinguisher, had put the brass nozzle back in the
frame, and then had poked it repeatedly with his finger, heart thumping,
whispering: 'Come on and hurt me. Come on and hurt me, you cheap
prick. Can't do it, can you? Huh? You're nothing but a cheap fire hose.
Can't do nothing but lie there. Come on, come on!' He had felt insane
with bravado. And nothing had happened. It was only a hose after all, only
canvas and brass, you could hack it to pieces and it would never complain,
never twist and jerk and bleed green slime all over the blue carpet, because
it was only a hose, not a nose and not a rose, not glass buttons or satin
bow, not a snake in a sleepy doze … and he had hurried on, had hurried
on because he was

('late, I'm late,' said the white rabbit.)

the white rabbit. Yes. Now there was a white rabbit out by the
playground, once it had been green but now it was white, as if something
had shocked it repeatedly on the snowy, windy nights and turned it old …

Danny took the passkey from his pocket and slid it into the lock.

(King 2011: 239–40)

One of the most distinctive and disorienting part of this scene is the plurality of voices, which cannot easily be traced to identifiable sources. In other
words, the construal is not consistently grounded from an easily identifiable
perspective throughout the extract.

Initially the scene is construed through Danny's perspective. This is made
clear through some of the noun profiles used – he describes, for example, the
'Presidential Sweet' (Presidential suite) – and the evaluative and modalized
language that signal his subjective account of events: 'There was nothing,
really nothing, in this hotel that *could* hurt him, and if he *had to* prove that
to himself by going into this room, *shouldn't* he do so?' While Danny subjectively construes the scene at this stage, he does seem detached from his
surroundings. He stares at the door with a 'drugged avidity', and there are
words of estrangement ('his upper body *seemed to* twitch and jiggle beneath
his flannel shirt'), which suggest that he is at the mercy of external forces.
Within this scene, as a whole, Danny is an agent in only two constructions –
the sentences that book-end the passage:

- Danny was standing outside room 217 again.
- Danny took the passkey from his pocket and slid it into the lock.

He is assigned mover and agent roles elsewhere ('he had hurried on'/'he had poked it repeatedly') but these actions are grounded in a different time (when he had 'stopped by the fire extinguisher'). In part what makes this scene seem non-cohesive is that there are multiple different grounded events being described here: (1) when Danny is outside the room and unlocks the door; (2) when he had visited the 'Presidential Sweet' and stopped by the fire extinguisher and (3) when he was 'out by the playground'. The shift in time zones means that our attention is pulled in multiple directions, contributing to the sense of disorientation created in this scene.

As the passage progresses, other voices become apparent – and the representation of Danny's thought and the speech/thoughts of the other speakers become blurred. This is because the ground of each speech event is unclear, and the speaker/hearer roles in the discourse event are equally ambiguous. Is Danny thinking, speaking or hearing these thoughts? Though the speech is partly bound by speech marks ('Lou, Lou, skip to m'Lou …'), the other turns are left unbound, with no inverted commas or reporting clause to indicate the ground of the speaker. There are other graphological markers, however, which impact on our conceptualization of the discourse. Italics, parentheses (used to frame an aside, in other contexts) and paragraph breaks are used to indicate multiple speaker turns:

> (*Curiosity killed the cat my dear redrum, redrum my dear, satisfaction brought him back safe and sound, from toes to crown; from head to ground he was safe and sound. He knew that those things*)
> (*are like scary pictures, they can't hurt you, but oh my god*)
> (*what big teeth you have grandma and is that a wolf in a BLUEBEARD suit or a BLUEBEARD in a wolf suit and I'm so*)
> (*glad you asked because curiosity killed that cat and it was the HOPE of satisfaction that brought him*)

The representation of these turns complicate the discourse context of this scene, and also our conceptualization of the number of speakers. In terms of topics, the plus frames – the ongoing discourse – follows directly on from the previous turn, the minus frame, almost as if the same speaker is continuing his or her train of thought ('*but oh my god*)/(*what big teeth you have grandma*'). Equally, these usage events seem to occur at non transition relevance places (parts of a conversation where a new speaker can contribute to the interaction; for example, at the end of a sentence, or in response to a question). We might expect that the question '*is that a wolf in a BLUEBEARD suit or a BLUEBEARD in a wolf suit*' would be followed by a break and a new turn with the response '*I'm so glad you asked*', for example, but this is not the case. Arguably, the conflation of these ideas and the continuation of the same sentence topic suggest an accord between the voices – as if there is a chorus of voices around Danny thinking and speaking in unison. While these statements are ambiguously grounded from other speakers' perspectives, Danny's subjective construal is reasserted at certain points (*'He knew that those things')/(are like scary pictures'*) as though he is trying to fight to make his thoughts/voice heard.

Another unsettling aspect of this scene is apparent in the semantic profiles that are drawn on. This scene focuses mainly on five-year-old Danny, and consequently the domain of CHILDHOOD is drawn on through references to fairy tales (*Little Red Riding Hood*) and other children's narratives (*Alice in Wonderland*), and children's rhymes ('Skip to my Lou') and proverbs ('curiosity killed the cat'). At the same time, however, the semantic profiles used by the 'voices' draws on the domain of VIOLENCE, through the references to violent folktales (*Bluebeard*), the use of expletives ('you cheap prick'), and descriptions of violent acts ('you could hack it to pieces and it would never complain'). Further, there are disconcerting points of connection between these two domains (the description of the 'big teeth' of the wolf; the fact that the rabbit had turned white from shock), which further complicate our conceptualization of the discourse.

7.5 Further activities

1.

Text 7E is an extract from the beginning of Myla Goldberg's (2003) experimental short story 'Comprehension Test'. Before you read the extract, consider these pieces of information in light of your discourse expectations:

  1 What style features would you expect to see in an experimental narrative?

  2 As mentioned, the title is 'Comprehension Test'. What does this suggest about the content, structure or style of the short story, if anything?

Now, read the extract below and consider the further questions that follow.

Text 7E

After reading each of the following passages, answer the questions to the best of your ability.

> We can truly observe America's great melting pot in action in this urban neighbourhood which, over the years, has been home to many of America's newest arrivals. As the tides of immigration have shifted, it too has changed.

Yet, like a chalkboard upon which yesterday's lesson has been only partially erased, its streets still bear traces of those who came before. Fifty years ago, this neighbourhood was home to scores of Eastern European Jews fleeing persecution. Over time, however, Chinese characters have appeared on buildings beside Hebrew ones. What once could have been described as an urban *shtetl* has become part of Chinatown.

Shops sell ginger root, dried mushrooms, and preserved duck eggs. Wheeled carts dispense one-dollar cartons of lo mein rice and noodles. An old man sets up his sidewalk stand, resoling Chinese sandals with used tire rubber. Yet around the corner, a row of electronics stores is still staffed by Orthodox Jews with their sidelocks and skull caps. A pickle store still vends its wares in briny barrels.

Though the words RABBI LOEW SCHOOL FOR BOYS are engraved in stone upon this building's façade, it is now an apartment building filled with Chinese families. Dr Lin's ground floor office neighbours the very playground he visited as a child. By the time Dr Lin's children are grown, this neighbourhood will have changed again, but one thing is certain: additions to our great melting pot are what help make America The Beautiful.

1   Dr Lin was shot to death in his office on Friday afternoon. Had he

   a   Ever felt uneasy in his office?

   b   Known his assailant?

   c   Attempted to defend himself?

   d   Pleaded for his life?

   e   Cried out for help?

2   Dr Lin's murderer successfully fled. Is it more likely that his shots

   a   Went unheard?

   b   Were assumed to be the sound of a car backfiring?

   c   Were shrugged off as someone else's problem?

   d   Went unreported for fear of criminal reprisal?

   e   Went unreported for fear of the law?

3   Were the shots fired

   a   In anger?

   b   In fear?

   c   In desperation?

   d   In revenge?

   e   In confusion?

4 As a policeman cordoned off the crime scene with POLICE LINE DO
   NOT CROSS tape, did he feel

   a Important?

   b Sad?

   c Annoyed?

   d Angry?

   e Nothing?

*[Two NEIGHBOURHOOD RESIDENTS approach a sign that has been posted
on the gate fronting Dr Lin's office. A police sketch appears below the word
WANTED. Beside the poster, a scrap of yellow police tape remains tied to
the fence. The two men talk while facing the poster.]*

RESIDENT 1: Did you know him?
RESIDENT 2: No. I passed by yesterday on my way home, but I did not stop.
RESIDENT 1: I came as soon as I heard the sirens, but I didn't see anything.
RESIDENT 2: Today I was expecting for police to be everywhere, but there is
     nothing.

(Goldberg 2003: 1–2)

3 How does this story manipulate the CDS established between writer
   and reader? What effect does this have on the experience of reading
   this story?

4 Does this story seem cohesive to you? How are reference point relationships formed in this text?

5 What other style choices contribute to the categorization of this story
   as an experimental text? Are there any other concepts from cognitive
   grammar that might help us to analyse its distinctive style?

2.

Choose a film narrative that you know well (e.g. your favourite film, or the last
one that you saw) and consider the following questions. It might help to start by
thinking about the opening scene, in particular, in order to focus the analysis:

1 What viewing frames were established in the opening of the film?
   What was the focus of the scene?

2 Are there any multimodal or nonlinguistic cues that impact on how
   the focus of the exchange is presented to the audience?

3 Were you aware of the ground of the discourse event (i.e. was it
   focused through a particular character's perspective?)

4   Did this impact on the way you perceived the relationship between the plus and minus frames of the narrative?

5   To what extent did the film rely on the fictive simulation (see Chapter 5) of events?

6   To what extent was shared knowledge/wider (extra-textual) context, required to experience the fictional world? Did this vary throughout the narrative?

3.

In groups, divide up the content chapters of this book (2–7). Pick one or two of the key ideas presented in the chapter and prepare answers to the following questions:

1   How might you go about carrying out macro-level stylistic analyses of this grammatical phenomenon? It may be helpful to think about this in relation to the analysis of a particular text.

2   Does scaling up the cognitive grammar framework for discourse-level analyses present any problems or challenges, in your opinion?

3   If you have identified problems, how might these be overcome? If not, what makes cognitive grammar work successfully for discourse-level application?

7.6 Further reading

The original work of Langacker does not broach the topic of discourse applications in any depth. While some of the key ideas presented in this chapter are addressed in Langacker (2008), the examples offered do not tend to consider units of language bigger than a few sentences. Taylor (2002) goes into greater detail about constructions and idiomatic expressions but similarly does not consider examples above the level of the sentence. Of course, as this chapter has argued, any stylistic tool should ideally be able to account for both micro- and macro-patterns of language. Stockwell's (2009) account of reference points and 'atmosphere' presents a convincing example of how reference point relationships can be scaled across a text and how they can be built to create a particular literary 'texture'. This analysis combines force dynamics, profiling and 'dominion tracing' to consider how specific schematic knowledge is evoked and revoked within the extract. Similarly, van Vliet's (2009) study also carries out a discourse-level application of reference point relationships. In particular, this paper draws on ideas from Text World Theory to consider anaphora in literary fiction. In addition, Harrison (2017a) begins to address how other key concepts from cognitive grammar (construal operations, grounding and the CDS, among others) can be scalable for stylistic application. Van Vliet's (2009) study and some of these ideas are also considered in Harrison et al. (2014). For a more detailed analysis of cognitive grammar in *Elizabeth Is Missing* (following Activity 7.2), see Harrison's (2017b) representation of Maud's episodic memory in the novel. Originally, the CDS was applied within the context of spoken conversation, specifically (see Langacker 1987, 2008). Cognitive grammar's CDS model is conceptually similar to the idea of the discourse world in Text World Theory (see Werth 1999; Gavins 2007; Gavins and Lahey 2016). The idea of the focus of an exchange is described in more detail by Harder (1996), who argues that linguistic structures can be thought of as sets of 'instructions'. For an overview of spoken discourse and pragmatics, see Levinson (1983) and Thomas (1995), and for more current research, see the *Journal of Pragmatics*. For stylistic applications of pragmatics, in particular, see Chapman and Clark (2014).

Chapter 8
Sample responses and additional activities

8.1 Structure of this chapter

This chapter contains sample responses for all the main activities in the book. We do not offer these responses as definitive answers but encourage you to use them as a way of stimulating your thinking in conjunction with your own ideas as you have worked through this book.

This chapter also has a set of additional texts and activities for each of Chapters 2–7. These are designed to further develop your expertise and confidence in using cognitive grammar as a method for stylistic analysis. We have also included some further discussion questions (Section 8.4) to allow you to examine and explore the affordances of cognitive grammar in stylistics in more detail. Finally, the end of the chapter provides a list of what we believe are the key texts you should read if you want to continue exploring both cognitive grammar and cognitive approaches to linguistic and literary study more generally.

8.2 Sample responses

Chapter 2 Conceptual Semantics

Activity 2.1: Exploring image schemas

The extract begins with the narrator representing his situation in terms of a CONTAINMENT schema; in this instance, of course, the narrator is inside his mother's body. Interestingly, the sense of being contained is coloured by a lack of understanding as to why he is in there. This is evident in the noun phrase with the general lexis 'a woman' and the pro-form 'who' instead of the more personal 'my mother'. Equally, the narrator's sense of direction draws on an orientation image schema 'upside down' as does his sense of time and moving in and out of states, 'in my careless youth'. The narrator's sense of space as a bounded area in which he is contained includes some understanding of the fact that it feels smaller as a result of his growth. Indeed, his biological growth from foetus to unborn child is conceptualized through a SOURCE-PATH-GOAL image schema. Words and phrases such as 'drifted', 'floated', 'slow-motion somersaults', 'colliding gently' and 'my private ocean' conceptualize the narrator as trajector moving along a path towards a goal (birth) and within the landmark of his mother's womb.

In the later part of the extract, the narrator's now fully inverted state gives rise to a further representation of the space he is in as 'crammed', with 'not an inch of space to myself'. Indeed, his sense of containment is actualized through the negative representation of the womb as 'the bloody walls'. In this instance the narrator (trajector) represents himself as spreading out to fill up the womb (landmark) so as to restrict his own sense of space.

Finally, the anticipation of the future is realized through integrating a SOURCE-PATH-GOAL schema, 'what awaits me' with a further CONTAINMENT schema, 'what might draw me in'. In the novel, a reworking of Shakespeare's *Hamlet*, the narrator later listens to his mother plotting to kill his father with the help of her lover, his uncle, the 'pillow-talk of deadly intent'. In this sense, the narrator anticipates his own birth into a world of crime and dishonesty. The irony (from a cognitive grammar perspective) is that all of the narration is taking place in the womb, thus presenting a literary representation of how image schemas emerge from (pre)birth.

Activity 2.3: Domains in poetry

In this poem, there are two pairs of domains that are evoked. First, 'hand', 'warm', 'blood' and 'veins' are understood against the background of the domains of a body and life. Second, 'icy', 'tomb', haunt' and 'chill' are understood against the background of the domains of death and, more explicitly, temperature. The poem works by drawing on the perceived contrast between these pairs of domains and between the current state of the hand (alive) and the imagined, projected state where the hand and presumably the speaker is dead. Indeed the speaker's desire to force the addressee of the poem to yearn for death and by consequence revitalize him inverts the structure of the domains. In this poem, the 'hand' has to be understood (unless we assign it some supernatural power) in relation to a body of which it is a part. This pushes us to assign some agency to the hand and make some sense of the desire of the speaker in order to attach meaning to the poem.

In fact, this poem, considered by many to be the final lines Keats wrote, has been variously interpreted as being penned to his lover Fanny Brawne (the poem either is angry towards her or celebrates her love for him in desiring her own death) or else consists of his final thoughts on the relationship between writing and reading poetry (the dead author is brought back to life by the reader through the re-animation that is the experience of reading poetry).

Activity 2.4: Metaphor in advertising

The advertisement draws explicitly on and primarily uses the metaphor LEADERSHIP IS A JOURNEY which in itself is an elaboration of the more general LIFE IS A JOURNEY metaphor. There is also the use of a second metaphor, IDEAS ARE PLANTS, realized through the expressions 'cross-pollinate ... diverse perspectives' and 'harvest ... collective discoveries'. These emphasize the collaborative nature of the course.

The main metaphor that conceptualizes a career as a series of movements along a path is realized in lexical choices such as 'become' and 'transformation process' and particularly through the supporting visual image of the staircase. The image depicts business executives moving up the staircase, presumably from a starting point (early career and/or pre-course) to an end point (later career and/or post-course), and clearly SOURCE-PATH-GOAL and MOTION image schemas underpin the visual realization of the metaphor.

The open door at the top of the staircase, representing the career high point and leading to a blue sky, perhaps evokes schematic knowledge of common idiomatic expressions such as 'reach high' and 'aim for the sky'. Indeed, the upwards movement depicted in the image draws on the orientational/spatial metaphors UP IS GOOD and UP IS POWERFUL in order to emphasize the benefits of the training course. The potential delegate (here the implied reader is a possibly young and certainly ambitious business executive) is positioned as being given the affordances to be able to escalate their career and reach a desired senior position more easily through attending the event.

Chapter 3 Construal

Activity 3.1: Exploring the effects of specificity in the ghost genre

The degrees of specificity that Connolly uses in this extract vary in interesting ways. First, the substance coming from the bathroom door is described in largely general ways, initially with the schematic 'something warm and sticky' and then the elaborations, 'stream of viscous liquid', 'clear liquid' and 'sticky paste' all of which have equivalent degrees of granularity that connote some sense of mystery and unknown and form a coherent chain across the extract. Equally, the generality of the room described through the lexical items 'bathroom' and 'lamp' reveal little actual detail and position the reader at a distance from a more finely grained view of the room that could be presented. This might be interpreted as helping to sustain a more supernatural atmosphere. In contrast, the more specific construals of Teal's physical attributes, his 'bare feet' and the 'cry' he gives in fear, provide a more focused and intense view of his situation.

When Teal views the supernatural entity, the way in which he is presented as kneeling down to look through the keyhole is mirrored in the elaborative relationship of lexical items that follows. The granularity that is physically rendered possible by Teal's looking through the keyhole is manifested in the construal of the entity that he sees, which moves from being described in very general terms to very specific ones, emphasizing the emerging horror of Teal's experience:

> A vague whiteness/the whiteness/the substance → scorched flesh/damp
> with sticky mucus/grey-green legs/ mottled with decay/distended stomach

The horror is such that Teal appears unable to construe what he has seen in more than the very general term 'body'. The effect is of a zooming out to capture a more schematic construal of the entity; the use of 'body' simply positions it as supernatural.

Activity 3.2: Progressive forms in poetry

In this extract, the verb 'plunges along' is a non-progressive form but almost all other instances that follow provide a restricted viewing frame and one that arguably affords a sense of closeness with the scene being described. For example, 'Spouting and frisking/Turning and twisting' affords only partial access to the movement of the waterfalls; the reader is placed in the middle of the scene, and one effect might be that it mimics the experiencing of the scene itself at the falls. This abundance of progressive forms is repeated across the whole poem so as to evoke the atmosphere of experiencing the beauty of this natural phenomenon. Indeed, the poem as a whole is set out in a way so that physically it mimics the physical flow of a waterfall. You can find the poem online and see for yourself how the organization of line lengths makes this work.

Activity 3.3: Identifying scope and profile

1   MS = human body; IS = arm/hand; P = finger
2   MS = human body; IS = arm/hand; P = knuckle
3   MS = building; IS = wall; P = door

4   MS = wall; IS = door; P = keyhole

5   MS = wall; IS = door; P = door hinge

6   MS = car; IS = dashboard; P = steering wheel

7   MS = United Kingdom; IS = South East England; P = London

8   MS = United Kingdom; IS = South East England; P = Kent

Activity 3.4: Attentional windowing in fiction

In this extract, the narrative path contains the boy and the girl jumping from the bridge into the Golden Gate strait (in San Francisco, United States). Although the initial portion of the path where the characters jump is windowed, most of the attention in the narrative is afforded to the medial portion as the characters descend and fall in love 'midair'. In fact the final portion is gapped possibly not only to avoid mentioning an unhappy ending but also (and more subtly) to draw attention to the tragic irony of the couple who fall in love just as they are about to die. The fact that the narrative contains only initial and medial windowing offers a darkly comic take (especially given the title of the story) on the absurdities involved with falling out of and in love.

Activity 3.5: Figure-ground and design

You could have commented on some of the following:

- Overall, the six Christmas decorations are placed as a type of composite figure against the general ground since they are sharply demarcated and defined and hence recognizable as forms standing out against the contrasting blurred background;

- Typically, the larger Christmas decoration is construed as figure against the remainder of the card since it is visually closer to us, although the viewer is able to alter this configuration by switching attention to a different decoration, which then becomes the figure in the scene;

- Within each of the decorations, certain aspects are figured against a more general ground. For example, in the largest decoration the horse and riders are naturally construed as the figure in terms of boldness (they are clearer than most of buildings, particularly those at the back), proximity (they appear closer in terms of viewing distance) and animation (we assume that they have moved, are moving or are able to move across the landscape).

Activity 3.6: Subjective and objective construal

In the extract from *Worst Fears*, the content is objectively construed. Although the narrator clearly provides a perspective on events and construes aspects in particular ways (e.g. the positioning implied by 'shoved the animal away' and 'Diamond ran round to the driver's side'), the narrator is not part of the scene being described and consequently feels detached from the action.

In the extract from *Embassytown*, however, the construal configuration is more complex. The content (the description of Embassytown and the narrator's memories there as a child) is subjectively construed but the use of 'we' (and then 'I') also places the subject of conception onstage as a participant in the scene being described and construed objectively. In this instance, the use of first-person pronouns denotes the dual role of the narrator/conceptualizer as subject and object of conception.

This blended perspective and construal where the narrating voice takes on the role of both subject and object of conception works well with the retrospective narrative technique. 'We' has as its referent the narrator at the time of narrating but also incorporates her (and others) at the time of the events in the past: this is also evident in the use of the past tense. Equally, the explicit vantage point taken by the narrator in the use of the verb of perception in the clause 'I see myself' offers a narration that highlights the conceptualized and perceived nature of the self and the split yet connected versions of the narrator's character are brought together through the act of remembering.

Of course, you could also say a great deal more about some of the other aspects of construal in this extract. For example, there are some interesting effects created by

- the clash between the non-specific lexis 'girls', 'boys' and 'children' rather than the use proper nouns which would provide greater identification of the characters and the more specific lexis of 'a steep-sloping backstreet of tenements', 'the smothered light of those old screens', 'a heavy two-sou piece', 'the library, the crenellations and armature' and 'the smooth plastone of its courtyard' all which combine to provide a richly imaginative fictional landscape;
- the spatial positioning from which a vantage point is adopted: the prepositional phrase patterning in 'by a particular house', 'beyond the rialto', 'in a steep-sloping backstreet of tenements', 'turned in colours', 'under the ivy';

- the windowing of attention which gives a broad panoramic sweep on the events being construed by offering a wide perspective;
- the figure-ground configuration in majority of clauses with 'I' or 'we' foregrounded as clausal subject.

Chapter 4   Nouns and Verbs

Activity 4.1: Profiling in poetry

1   Let me not to the marriage of true minds
2   Admit impediments. *Love* is not *love*
3   Which *alters* when it *alteration* finds,
4   Or bends with the *remover* to *remove*.

Many readers will be familiar with this sonnet, and will recognize the references to marriage vows ('Let me not to the marriage of true minds') and the attempt by the speaker to define love – one of the central preoccupations of the sonnet form. These observations have been well documented in the critical literature on the poem.

Though the previous example of the word 'fight' had, at its conceptual base, an event, in this poem the conceptual base of the word 'love' is presented as a state: one that is constant, inflexible and enduring. The first two underlined instances of the word profile noun schema. The 'X is not Y' syntactic construction conceptually profiles the noun schema, while simultaneously negating it. Consequently, two instances of love are presented: love as it should ideally be and the type of love that masquerades as the real thing (that 'bends with the remover to remove').

The defining differences between these two states are elaborated on in the construction on the next line. The alternating noun/verb schema profiles invite a reader to construe contrasting states of the same conceptual base. Line 3 profiles the word 'alter' in its two schematic forms: as a verb ('alters') and as a noun ('alteration'). Here, the conceptual base of the word is, inherently, an action: to alter something, or to undergo an alteration, intrinsically refers to a change of state. At the end of this line, the profiling of 'find' as a verb imbues 'love' with a sense of human agency (see introduction to agents and action chains in Chapter 5).

This pattern is paralleled in line 4, except here, the trajector of the action is profiled in the first instance ('the remover'). Again, the conceptual base of 'remove' signposts an event. In the first profile of this line, however, emphasis is placed on the one who performs the action rather than the outcome (in contrast to a noun schema of the event, as profiled through the word 'removal'). The prominence given to the trajector here reinforces the construal of 'love' as a state that has a degree of agency.

Activity 4.2: Scanning newspaper headlines

Trump *swings* the majority (perfective); May *leads* UK congratulations for the new president elect (perfective); Trump *is* victorious (imperfective); Trump's conversation with Farage *leaves* Britain leaders red-faced (perfective); Inside the mind of Theresa May (summary scan).

The perfective examples ('swings', 'leads', 'leaves') here are all scanned sequentially as each verb choice situates the headline description in relation to an ongoing, wider event.

The first headline, for example, signals a former sequence of events in which Trump did not hold the majority in the presidential campaign (as, conceptually speaking, 'swing' designates an entity that, either literally or figuratively, moves from one side to another). Although the second headline, 'May leads UK congratulations for the new president elect', profiles a particular part of the action – its beginning – the perfective form similarly indicates that this action is ongoing; and, based on the choice of verb, that others are currently following in May's footsteps.

The fourth example, 'Farage leaves Britain leaders red-faced', works similarly. The emphasis is on the outcome of the action ('leaves'), but again the perfective form allows us to sequentially access the rest of the event. The use of the perfective here helps us conceptualize that this is an ongoing state of affairs that, significantly, is yet to be resolved.

Conversely, the imperfective verb ('is') in the third example isolates just one state of Trump's overall campaign. Simply put the fact that 'Trump is victorious' profiles the final part of the event: the outcome. Consequently, this example is scanned summatively. It is a stative construction that simply outlines the fact declaratively.

The final example, 'Inside the mind of Theresa May' is likewise scanned summatively. In this headline, the absence of a verb profile means that we automatically conceptualize the information as a state. The preposition 'inside' acts as a placeholder for the verb but, since this is a preposition, it encodes a static, summative spatial relationship (compare, for example, how we would conceptualize this headline if we replaced this preposition with a verb such as 'accessing' or 'reading').

Activity 4.3: Reference points in children's fiction

As we would expect from a children's text for young readers, there is a lot of repetition in this text, and a clear relationship between the story text and the accompanying images.

It is apparent that the opening of this story is developed through a reference point chain: one that helps to orient, exactly, where and 'how the story begins'. The location of the 'dark dark hill' is the first reference point readers encounter, with the target 'the dark dark town' introduced in relation to this reference point through a prepositional relationship: 'On'. This spatial relationship is reinforced through the picture at the top of the first page of the story, which situates a town on a hill.

The rest of the text on the first page follows a clear syntactic pattern. Because of the repetition, each target becomes a reference point for the introduction of the next. This is reinforced graphologically – as each new target ('there was a dark dark town', line 3) forms the reference point and focus of the next new line of text ('In the dark dark town', line 4) – and also through the choice of determiners. As a target becomes reinstated as a reference point at the start of a new sentence, the determiner moves from the indefinite ('*a* dark dark house') to the definite ('*The* dark dark house').

In this way, a zooming in effect is created, which means that children's attention can be directed through particular features of the landscape in order to locate where 'some skeletons lived'. At first the skeletons are identified collectively, as a plural count noun grouped together through a proportional quantifier ('some'), before they are then singled out in turn and modified by size and shape: 'There was a big skeleton, a little skeleton and a dog skeleton'.

Activity 4.4: Reference points in metonymy

We understand this expression to describe the power of the written word over physical power (usually within the context of violence). Of course, neither 'writing' nor 'power/violence' is actually mentioned in this phrase. Instead, 'pen' and 'sword' act as reference points for these targets. We understand the 'pen' to represent a profile of the wider concept of writing, just as we know that the 'sword' here represents physical violence. In this way, we use these specific noun profiles ('pen', 'sword') as mental reference points in order to construe and comprehend the wider meaning of this phrase.

The cartoon, which was published in the aftermath of the Charlie Hebdo attacks in early 2015, reframes the idiom. The cartoonist Rob Tornoe has placed greater prominence on the 'pen' as a reference point by contextualizing an arsenal of writing/drawing utensils – not just one lone 'pen' – specifically located within the context of a battlefield. Here, the 'sword' is substituted by the reference point of a lone soldier holding a smoking gun. As with its written counterpart, the target of the cartoon is still easily construed. The targeted meaning of this particular cartoon, however, encompasses even more offstage implications than the written idiom. It draws conceptual equivalence between the power of artistic expression more generally, against the power held by terrorists within the current political climate.

Activity 4.5: Reference point chains in the opening of *Gone Girl*

Gone Girl (Flynn 2012) is a contemporary bestselling thriller that is centred on the character, Amy Dunne, and follows the police investigation in the aftermath of her disappearance. The novel has two narrators and splices between the two central protagonist perspectives: between diary entries from Amy in the lead-up to her disappearance, and her husband Nick's narrative of the events that follow her disappearance. Narratorial unreliability is present throughout the novel, and a brief analysis of this opening section shows how this unreliability can be explored through its specific stylistic choices.

The opening of the story is told through Nick's perspective, and this extract is framed as both a police report (as indicated through the emphatic title that suggests an account of 'NICK DUNNE' on 'THE DAY OF' the disappearance) and simultaneously as a first-person diary entry – or an interior monologue that is directed to Amy as the implied reader: 'What are you thinking? How are you feeling?' In this opening description of his wife, Nick appears to be focusing on Amy's head (her skull and her brain) rather than, as we might expect, providing a holistic description of what Amy looks like or her personality. It seems that one reference point for Amy – the thing that is most salient about her, from Nick's perspective – is this part of her body. Across the passage, he creates a reference point chain where he lists increasingly specific profiles: 'my wife' → 'her head' → 'the skull' → 'her mind' → 'her brain' → 'her thoughts'.

By isolating these particular reference points in order to describe Amy, Nick is describing his wife metonymically and anatomically. This description departs from the prototypical features of a romantic account of one's spouse, while simultaneously reinforcing a style feature associated with crime fiction: a preoccupation with body parts, and a dehumanization of victims. Furthermore, the noun phrases that form these targets change stylistically across the passage. Sometimes these targets are referred to through possessive constructions ('*my* wife', '*her* head', '*her* mind', '*her* thoughts'), which include Amy as a reference point within the description, and at other times Amy herself is backgrounded and instead these targets are introduced by definite determiner ('*the* back of *the* head', '*the* angles of it', '*the* skull'). This stylistic shift, coupled with the fact that Nick first refers to Amy as 'my wife' (her given name is not mentioned until the third paragraph) serves to objectify Amy, which, in turn, depersonalizes Nick's description of her and makes the commentary seem somewhat clinical. We might question: why is he describing her in this way?

Nominal compounds are used on three occasions. The first two – 'corn kernel' and 'riverbed fossil' – are introduced as targets to further describe the shape of Amy's head. Again, the fact that these nominal compounds are used as comparative reference points further emphasizes the objectification of Amy. The reference to 'riverbed fossil' is, at this stage of the novel, an evocative description. Given the fact that we know Amy to have disappeared at this point, we might pay more attention to the term 'fossil' – suggestive of something that has died. Equally, by being prefaced by the reference point and nominal compound 'riverbed', this whole phrase could possibly be read as foreshadowing what has happened to Amy.

Other negative collocates are referenced throughout the extract, particularly in the metaphorical choices. Nick describes 'unspooling' Amy's brain, which further signposts an attempt to objectify Amy – but in this comparison her thoughts are the target he wants to describe, in particular. These metaphorical comparisons continue when Nick likens Amy's thoughts to 'frantic centipedes', ones that he is trying to 'catch' and to 'pin down'.

The third compound – 'stormcloud' – combines two nouns to create a verb profile. To 'cloud' over something in itself as a verb profile is synonymous with 'hanging over' or possibly could be taken to mean obscuring something. With the 'storm' reference point, however, again a sense of foreboding is created. A storm cloud on the horizon both in its literal and figurative conceptualization indicates trouble ahead.

Chapter 5 Clauses

Activity 5.1: Setting the scene

With the exception of the two verb headers in the first sentence ('discovered' and 'moved'), all the clauses in this extract are stative clauses. While the verb 'lives' could be categorized as a dynamic verb in other contexts, here the narrator uses it to situate one entity in terms of another ('Miss Spink and Miss Forcible lived in the flat below Coraline's'). In other words, it is used to describe an existing state of affairs.

The high number of stative verbs means that the emphasis in this extract is on setting the scene; on establishing the facts and descriptors of this new fictional world. The predominance of stative clauses also means that the two dynamic clauses that are included are immediately foregrounded. Readers might assume from the outset, therefore, that Coraline's discovery of 'the door' is a significant event. At the same time, the lack of cognitive clauses means that, at this stage of the story, readers are not provided with an insight into the thoughts of Coraline. Instead, they are invited to construe this fictional world through the perspective of an external, offstage narrator – a typical stylistic feature of fairy-tale-style narratives – which outlines a more objective construal.

Activity 5.2: Identifying roles

1 The penguin (mvr) runs away (loc).

2 The penguin (zero) is asleep.

3 The penguin (ag) quickly (circ) passes the egg (istr) to another penguin (pt).

4 The penguin (exp) feels cold.

Activity 5.3: Roles in headlines

a In this sentence the noun phrase 'UK election results' is the agent that has impacted on the 'Brexit talks', the patient.

b In the first clause of the first sentence, Mervyn Wheatley holds an agent role: he is the source of the energy, and the one carrying out the action – while 'his yacht' is a patient, as it undergoes a change of state. In the second clause, Mervyn is not explicitly mentioned, but becomes a patient as he is at the receiving end of the second action within the sentence – the rescuing – performed by the agent,

Figure 8.1 Archetypal roles in penguins

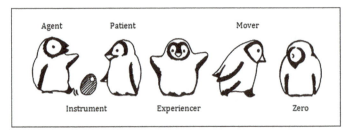

'the Queen Mary 2'. This second clause is a passive construction (see Section 5.6.1).

c 'The concert' is a stimulus within the context of this next clause; and 'the nation' is an experiencer. This is because the verbs in the clause, 'heartened' and 'cheered', describe emotive processes – or, to use the terminology introduced at the beginning of Chapter 5, because a cognitive clause is depicted. Clauses with verbs of emotion/cognition are said to function in a similar way to canonical events, like those represented in a) and b). The stimulus is seen to work in a similar way to agents, and the experiencers also adopt patient-like roles. This difference between verbs of action and verbs of cognition is explored in further detail in Section 5.5.1.

d The final example is a stative clause and a zero role is outlined. A property is shown – Hamilton winning the race – but there are no interactions between entities within the clause. 'Winner' is therefore a noun complement. In other words, 'winner' takes on a more adjective-like role within this sentence (as compared to, for example, a sentence like 'the trophy was given to the winner' – where the noun phrase instead is clearly a participant in the grammatical process).

Activity 5.4: Movement in texts

a In this opening extract to *I Capture the Castle*, the emphasis is on 'capturing' the scene and on providing details about the space and orientation of the fictional world. Where agency and motion is assigned, it is mainly attributed to parts of the landscape: the 'drips' of water are movers, and the 'ploughed fields' are similarly ascribed movement through the verb profile 'stretch'. This is known as 'fictive motion' (see Talmy 2000a, b) in that, while the clause describes an ongoing, stative fact, the verb choice nevertheless suggests dynamicity. The final clause also designates a move to the participant role within a motion event, albeit one which is modalized: 'spring will surge'.

Other clauses, however, are stative, featuring zero participant roles: 'the view ... is excessively drear '; 'the ruined walls' are 'on the edge of the moat'; 'the rain ... is good for nature'. There are also numerous locative descriptions, as outlined through the numerous prepositional constructions that provide extra circumstantial information: 'from', 'into', 'by', 'through'; 'Beyond' (X2); 'on' (X2), 'to'. These prepositional relationships create the impression of a 'through-view' perspective: the narrator is telling us all she can see through her static position. Further, as this is a diary entry, the narrator also sets herself as both agent and patient for this description: '*I* tell *myself*'. Similarly, readers are included as patients subject to the external forces of nature: 'spring will surge on *us*'.

b   Like with the first extract, this second extract from a science book similarly does not display heightened motion. The extract mainly describes an ongoing state of affairs in the cosmos and is descriptive, but it seems to be emphasizing the separation between facts of which scientists are sure, and those about which they remain uncertain.

The opening sentence casts the stars as a zero role participant ('The stars are tiny specks'), while in contrast, they are represented as agents in the second sentence: they are said to 'exhibit no extravagant loops on the sky', but the use of negation here is interesting. Since the stars are *not* actually performing an action, schematically speaking, the agency of the verb 'exhibit' is both attributed to and removed from the stars at the same time. This occurs again later with the clause that describes how the stars 'appear to be'. The modalization in 'appear' and the verb phrase 'to be' again casts the stars in a zero participant role. These participant roles emphasize the fact that they are 'feature-less' and seemingly 'immobile' and unreachable.

Scientists/humans are cast as powerless to verify facts about the cosmos through the stative clause and zero participant role designated by, the again negated, construction 'we have no telescope capable' of providing further information. This lack of knowledge is contrasted with more exacting locative information brought about by preposi-tional construction ('Beyond the nightly circular arcs'), but continue to be given minimal agency. The final sentence casts us as experi-encers, and the 'distance' between stars as the stimulus, and further bookends the description with a declarative, categorical construction: 'And yet we know the distance to each and every one'.

c   This third passage from *The Curious Incident* presents clearer and more straightforward action chains than the previous two extracts. With the exception of the zero roles in the clauses 'Father was still at work' and the identifying 'one of the things was this book', Christopher Boone (the narrating protagonist) initiates the agent, mover and experiencer roles in the clause constructions in this extract.

His role as a mover is represented through the repeated verb 'went' ('went inside'; 'went into the kitchen'; 'went through to the living room') and these clauses of movement provide clear information about his change in location. The other actions in which Christopher performs an agent role are all dynamic ones: 'unlocked', 'took off', 'put', 'taken', 'show', 'made', 'heated'. The patients in these sentences are the objects inside the house with which he is interacting: he unlocks 'the front door'; takes off his 'coat'; puts 'his things' on the table; makes 'a raspberry milkshake' and so on.

This simple list-like style of this extract exemplifies the default viewing arrangement of clause creation: Christopher is commenting on and communicating, as directly as possible, his experiences with the world. The sequential ordering of events and the syndetic structuring of the clauses is characteristic of Christopher's distinctive world view in the novel.

Activity 5.5: Action in dystopian fiction

Below are some of the ideas you might have commented on in your responses:

The pace is increased by the presence of: short clause structures ('She never misses'); exclamative constructions ('And I've missed it!'); strong cohesive connections, with conjunctions linking new clauses with previous sentences ('Then the boy slips to the ground'); high-action verb profiles ('lunge', 'scoop', 'sprint', 'grapple', 'stagger', 'running', 'clutching', 'sling', etc.); and corresponding predominance of mover/agent roles ('I lunge', 'I stagger', 'I sling', etc.).

In addition to the high energy motion verbs and mover roles, there are examples of epistemic modality as Katniss is cast in experiencer roles: 'I think'; 'I've been feeling'; 'I can hear'; 'Somehow I know', etc. These create a sense of disorientation and uncertainty in places.

The narrative moves between the subjective and objective construal in tandem with the presence/absence of modality. The movement between the conceptualizer and the object of conceptualization increases the tension, and foregrounds those clauses that are more categorically represented: 'And I'm her next target'.

Many examples of non-human participants in both agent and patient roles (in italics) and also examples of metonymy as body parts are used as participants (in bold below):

- **My feet** shuffle for a moment, confused at the direction **my brain** wants to take
- splattering **my face** with blood
- That's when I see *the knife* in **his back**
- **one hand** clutching *a half-dozen knives*
- I can hear *the blade* whistling towards me

- I reflexively hike *the pack* up to protect **my head**
- I sling *the pack* over **one shoulder**
- *The blade* lodges in *the pack*
- *Adrenaline* shoots through me
- *A grin* crosses **my face**

This deferral of agency and motion from human participants in their entirety and to body parts creates a sense of detachment and objectivity in the act of killing in this scene. It also increases the sense of confusion by isolating smaller parts of the immediate scope (see Chapter 3) of the scene rather than the scene in its entirety – as if the events of the scene are too traumatic and occurring too quickly for the narrator to take in as a whole.

Chapter 6 Grounding

Activity 6.1: Identifying grounding elements for nouns

The grounding elements are in italics.

1   *The* bridge was open to traffic
2   Have you read *this* book?
3   Some of *the* players were not happy with *the* referee's decision
4   *Each* customer received *a* refund
5   *No* warning was given
6   Can I buy you *a* drink?

Some grounding elements are definite: e.g. 'the'
Some grounding elements are indefinite: e.g. 'a'
Some grounding elements quantify: e.g. 'each', 'no'
Some grounding elements are demonstratives: e.g. 'this'

Activity 6.2: Grounding in *Dracula*

In this extract, Harker uses a series of nominals that are grounded largely through the use of the definite article, for example:

- 'the crowd'
- 'the inn door'

- 'the sign of the cross'
- 'the evil eye'

In these instances, each expression profiles a specific instance of a type; the definite article suggests that each noun is one of a kind and easily recognizable to both the implied narratee of the novel and the reader. Here the specific nature of each relates to the storyworld that we have built up and are following and the immediacy of the situation; the use of 'the' might also makes the narrative feel familiar and close to us as readers. In contrast, less definite instances are used when simply relaying information about other things in the narrative world.

- 'a considerable size'
- 'a fellow passenger'
- 'a charm or guard'

Finally, the narrative is told in the past tense. The clausal grounding signals out instances of each process and positions them in relation to the context of the narrative itself and the situation we find ourselves in as readers of the novel looking back on events that are relayed as having happened in the past.

Activity 6.3: Nominal grounding in non-fiction

In the first sentence, there is extensive use of overt grounding with the definite article 'the', used to single out unique referents that the reader's attention is drawn towards. Pullinger uses one of these, 'The prison', anaphorically to refer back to a referent that is likely to have been mentioned already in the discourse, while the indirect grounding in 'their cottages' also acts as a way of ensuring discourse cohesion. Later, there are examples of intrinsic grounding through the use of proper nouns such as 'Gallow Field Road' and 'HMP Gartree', which help to provide a specific spatial location and set of parameters for Pullinger's following narrative. The use of indefinite grounding elements 'a' and 'an' in the nominals 'a dark walled-in council estate' and 'an iron door', 'a small room' activate spaces for new information to be fed into the narrative.

Once the ROOM frame has been activated, and is part of the current discourse shared by writer and reader, parts of it can be referred to through the use of the definite article, for example 'the other side of the glass'. In a similar way, the introduced PRISON frame allows for overt grounding with a definite article to refer to 'the men', 'the prisoners' and 'the officers', so that the scene being presented to the reader appears to be easily identifiable and conceptually close. The complex nominal (here a heavily pre-modified noun phrase) 'an elaborately hierarchical, coded, masculine world' demonstrates how the role of the grounding element is to complete the nominal; the order of the three adjectives is also iconically motivated since the position of 'masculine' next to the noun 'world' reflects the emphasis given to the world of the prison in terms of its male population and sense of masculine behaviours and values.

Finally, there are examples of zero-form grounding where the lack of a covert grounding element focuses attention and interpretative significance instead on the frames associated with the referents 'rambling roses' and 'privileged temporary access'.

Activity 6.4: Reference in 'Meeting at night'

One of the most interesting aspects of this poem is the contrast in the use of definite reference between the two stanzas. The nominals in stanza 1 are almost entirely grounded through the use of the definite article. The only exceptions are 'fiery ringlets' and 'pushing prow' (zero-forms), and 'its speed' (indirect grounding through possessive determiner). In this stanza, the majority of the referents are profiled as unique; one possible interpretation of this is that it makes the scene being described feel closer to the reader, who adopts a singular focused perspective and a rich awareness of the entities that are profiled in each of the nominals.

In stanza 2, the pattern is more complex. In this stanza the speaker has left the boat and is travelling across land to where a meeting with his/her lover will take place. We can categorize the nominals in this stanza as follows:

- 'a mile': indefinite article
- 'warm sea-scented beach': zero-form
- 'three fields': numeral
- 'a farm': indefinite article
- 'a tap': indefinite article
- 'the pane': definite article
- 'the quick sharp scratch': definite article
- 'blue spurt': zero-form
- 'a lighted match': indefinite article
- 'a voice': indefinite article
- 'its joys and fears': indirect grounding through possessive
- 'the two hearts': definite article

The more extensive use of indefinite reference in this stanza reflects the new surroundings that mark the speaker's journey across unknown territory. Indefinite articles select from a set to activate space for new information to be introduced into the narrative. Of particular importance in this stanza is the nominal 'a farm' in the second line that activates a space from which the remainder of the action in the stanza is conceptualized and understood. The definiteness of 'the pane' and 'the quick sharp scratch' profiles unique referents, again possibly conveying a sense of conceptual closeness, whereas zero-form grounding in 'blue spurt' draws attention to the colour of 'a lighted match' (although interestingly the grounding element is indefinite) and its associations rather than any sense of determinacy. This is also phonologically foregrounded through the juxtaposition of the voiced (b)/voiceless (p) bilabial plosives.

Finally, indefinite reference is used to activate a space for the lover to have 'a voice' before the poem ends with the definite article grounding the noun phrase 'two hearts'. Here, the speaker assumes the uniqueness of the referents, understood in the context of the climax of the poem where the lovers now embrace, means that definite reference can now be used.

Activity 6.5: Types and forms of modality

1 Boulomaic modality, modal lexical verb

2 Epistemic modality, modal auxiliary verb

3 Deontic modality, modal auxiliary verb

4 Epistemic modality, modal adjective

5 Epistemic modality, modal adverb

6 Dynamic modality, modal auxiliary verb

7 Epistemic modality, modal auxiliary verb

8 Epistemic modality, modal auxiliary verb

9 Deontic modality, modal auxiliary verb

10 Epistemic modality, modal clause

Activity 6.6: Degrees of modality

In this extract, there are three uses of the epistemic modal auxiliary verb 'may', which express relatively weak assertion and ground the situations they describe in potential reality. The narrator's use of this modal form suggests that they are extremely uncertain and lack concrete knowledge regarding the state of affairs about to be described in the story. Since this is the beginning of the short story, the reader might view the narrator's uncertainty as a sign of unreliability and therefore treat the subsequent relaying of narrative events with some caution and scepticism.

Given the genre of the story, we might even expect to be presented with a fictional mind that is anxious and doubtful. In this instance, the dominant modal pattern (weakly asserted epistemic modality) is suggestive of a bewildered and self-questioning consciousness. Of course, the genre is also foregrounded through the use of discrete lexical choices such as 'madness' and 'haunted', and the noun phrases 'intense suffering' and 'sixth sense', which highlight intrigue, mystery and the supernatural.

Chapter 7 Discourse

Activity 7.1: Spoken discourse in *Big Bang Theory*

The focus of the two main interlocutors here (Penny and Sheldon) is not shared initially. While both speakers are contributing turns that comments on a shared viewing frame – Penny asks if she can 'start' eating the takeaway (turn 1), whereas Sheldon replies by shifting the focus to his 'spot' on the sofa (turn 2).

The rhetorical question in turn 5 ('What's the difference?') would not necessarily lead to a full explanation in response, but nevertheless initiates one (as Sheldon contributes in turn 8). Thus there is a mismatch between the minus and anticipated frames of the discourse event here, which makes this exchange largely non-collaborative.

The tension here exists in the fact that, though the physical context of the speakers in the scene is the same, the shared knowledge between the speakers is not. As recent acquaintances, Penny is unaware of Sheldon's spot on the sofa, the reasons why it makes a 'difference' where he sits, and of his personality in general. The response to a rhetorical question, for example, would not be anticipated in other discourse contexts, but nevertheless is provided by Sheldon here. Furthermore, the fact that Sheldon retains a focus on his seat on the sofa is an indication that he wishes to retain his spot; a discourse goal that is not acknowledged by Penny until turn 9 ('Do you want me to move?').

Activity 7.2: Meaning-making

To circumnavigate her memory gaps, in these noun phrases Maud relies on descriptions of an object's schematic properties. Each referent is given greater prominence through the fact that it is not labelled directly; and instead, a series of targets is listed that cluster around the lacuna of the actual name (a toaster, a tie and a packet of pencils, respectively). Often Maud's descriptions include repeated labels (*'bread*-heater, the *bread* browner'; 'a packet of *lamp posts,* tiny *lamp posts'*), or explicitly rule out potential possibilities (*'not a* scarf, *not a* cravat'). Here Maud's under-specification, also known in stylistics as under-lexicalization, is a characteristic feature of her memory loss. Additionally, these underspecified descriptions function to make Maud's construal more subjective.

The prominence of Maud's subjective position continuously reminds a reader of Maud's unreliability throughout the novel. This sets up a layered construal that is at the centre of reading this text. As in the case of the three underspecified references listed here, for example, readers are placed in the position of providing the missing information themselves, from their extra-textual knowledge. This therefore invites a reader to maintain an awareness of their own understanding of events alongside the construal of events as described by the narrator. In CDS terms, the 'shared knowledge' between reader and character-narrator has points of contact, but does not entirely overlap. This establishes and emphasizes Maud's forgetfulness; setting her up as a very unlikely protagonist for a detective quest.

8.3 Further activities

8.3.1 Chapter 2 Conceptual semantics

Spatial prepositions: The construction of character and place
Text 8A is the opening to 'Careful', a short story by Raymond Carver. It makes extensive use of spatial prepositions in its construction of characters and place.

Text 8A

After a lot of talking – what his wife, Inez, called assessment – Lloyd moved out of the house and into his own place. He had two rooms and a bath on the top floor of a three-story house. Inside the rooms, the roof slanted down sharply. If he walked around, he had to duck his head. He had to stop to look from his windows and be careful getting in and out of bed. There were two keys. One key let him into the house itself. Then he climbed some stairs that passed through the house to a landing. He went up another flight of stairs to the door of his room and used the other key on that lock.

Once, when he was coming back to his place in the afternoon, carrying a sack with three bottles of André champagne and some lunch meat, he stopped on the landing and looked into his landlady's living room. He saw the old woman lying on her back on the carpet. She seemed to be asleep. Then it occurred to him that she might be dead. But the TV was going, so he chose to think she was asleep. He didn't know what to make of it. He moved the sack from one arm to the other. It was then that the woman gave a little cough, brought her hand to her side, and went back to being quiet and still again. Lloyd continued on up the stairs and unlocked his door. Later that day, towards evening, as he looked from his kitchen window, he saw the old woman down in the yard, wearing a straw hat and holding her hand against her side. She was using a little watering can on some pansies.

(Carver [1983] 2003: 103)

1 Highlight all of the spatial prepositions that you can find in this extract. What do you notice?

2 Now trace how Carver utilizes these prepositions and their trajector-landmark configurations as the extract progresses, drawing on your knowledge of image schemas. What do you find significant about the way that these operate as the extract develops?

Containment image schemas in a Shakespearean soliloquy

Text 8B is a soliloquy from the end of Act 1, scene 2 of *King Henry the Fourth Part One*. Prince Hal, the heir to the throne, is renowned for spending his time with low-life companions, a reputation which angers his father, King Henry. At this point in the play, Hal demonstrates his awareness of others' perception of him and vows to abandon his lifestyle. He also tells the audience that he will display his true identity when and as he sees fit so as to give the impression of a remarkable transformation. This soliloquy is thus an important moment in the tetralogy of plays that charts his rise from wayward prince to king and anticipates the events of *King Henry the Fourth Part Two* when Hal rejects Falstaff, the most famous and influential of his companions once he becomes king.

Text 8B

PRINCE
I know you all, and will awhile uphold
The unyoked humour of your idleness:
Yet herein will I imitate the sun,
Who doth permit the base contagious clouds
To smother up his beauty from the world,
That, when he please again to be himself,
Being wanted, he may be more wondered at,
By breaking through the foul and ugly mists
Of vapours that did seem to strangle him.

If all the year were playing holidays,
To sport would be as tedious as to work;
But when they seldom come, they wished-for come,
And nothing pleaseth but rare accidents.
So when this loose behaviour I throw off
And pay the debt I never promised,
By how much better than my word I am,
By so much shall I falsify men's hopes;
And, like bright metal on a sullen ground,
My reformation, glittering o'er my fault,
Shall show more goodly and attract more eyes
Than that which hath no foil to set it off.
I'll so offend to make offence a skill,
Redeeming time when men think least I will.

(*1H4* 1.2.184–207)

1 Examine how Hal draws on a CONTAINMENT image schema throughout this soliloquy. What elaborations of the basic pattern can you see?

2 How are these image schemas used to present the message Hal wants the audience to understand and to project his sense of self-image and identity?

8.3.2 Chapter 3 Construal

Construal and characterization

The following extracts are two examples of openings that present particular construals of characters and settings. Text 8C is from the beginning of Neil Gaiman's novel *The Ocean at The End of The Lane*. Text 8D is the opening to 'Edward the Conqueror', a short story by Roald Dahl.

Text 8C

I wore a black suit and a white shirt, a black tie and black shoes, all polished and shiny: clothes that normally would make me feel uncomfortable, as if I were in a stolen uniform, or pretending to be an adult. Today they gave me comfort, of a kind. I was wearing the right clothes for a hard day.

(Gaiman 2013: 1)

1 Which descriptive elements of the scene are profiled in this extract? What is the conceptual base of these profiles?

2 Does this construal seem more objective or subjective?

3 Considering this is the opening paragraph to the novel, how does this description impact upon the characterization of the narrator?

Text 8D

Louisa, holding a dishcloth in her hand, stepped out of the kitchen door at the back of the house into the cool October sunshine.

'Edward!' she called. '*Ed-ward*! Lunch is ready!'

She paused a moment, listening; then she strolled out on to the lawn and continued across it – a little shadow attending her – skirting the rose bed and touching the sundial lightly as she went by. She moved rather gracefully for a woman who was small and plump, with a tilt in her walk and a gentle swinging of the shoulders and the arms. She passed under the mulberry tree on to the brick path, then went all the way along the path until she came to the place where she could look down into the dip at the end of the large garden.

'*Edward*! Lunch!'

She could see him now, about eighty yards away, down in the dip on the edge of the wood – the tallish narrow figure in khaki slacks and dark green sweater, working beside a big bonfire with a fork in his hands, pitching brambles on to the top of the fire. It was blazing fiercely, with orange flames and clouds of milky smoke, and the smoke was drifting back over the garden with a wonderful scent of autumn and burning leaves.

Louisa went down the slope towards her husband. Had she wanted, she could easily have called again and made herself heard, but there was something about a first-class bonfire that impelled her towards it, right up close so that she could feel the heat and listen to it burn.

(Dahl [1953] 1979: 263)

1 Comment on anything in this extract that you find interesting in terms of the cognitive grammar notions of specificity and scope. For example, what can you say about the description of Edward standing by and working on the bonfire?

2 Look at the way that figure-ground configuration works in this extract. Starting at the beginning, highlight which aspect(s) is positioned as figure and which as ground. When and how does this change as the story progresses?

3 What vantage points are assumed by Louisa and the reader as conceptualizers of the narrative events? How are these lexically and grammatically realized? What can you say about how perspective operates in this extract?

8.3.3 Chapter 4 Nouns and verbs

Nouns and verb profiles in experimental fiction

Text 8E is taken from the contemporary experimental text, *Grief Is the Thing with Feathers*, considered to be part-prose, part-poetry. In this text, a crow (representing grief) visits a father, who is mourning the recent loss of his wife, and his two young sons. The point of view moves between the father, the boys and the crow.

The extract below is taken from early in the text when the crow first visits the family, and is narrated from the crow's perspective. This passage is unusual in that it seems simultaneously both cohesive and non-cohesive, and part of this is that many of the lexical choices here are re-appropriations of familiar phrases.

Text 8E

Very romantic, how we first met. Badly behaved. Trip trap. Two-bed upstairs flat, spit-level, slight barbed-error, snuck in easy through the wall and up the attic bedroom to see those cotton boys silently sleeping, intoxicating hum of innocent children, lint, flack, gack-pack-nack, the whole place was heavy mourning, every surface dead Mum, every crayon, tractor, coat, welly, covered in a film of grief. Down the dead Mum stairs, plinkety plink curled claws whisper, down to Daddy's recently Mum-and-Dad's bedroom. I was Herne the hunter hornless, funt. Munt. Here he is. Out. Drunk-for-white. ... He was an accidental remnant and I knew this was the best gig, a real bit of fun. I put my claw on his eyeball and weighed up gouging it out for fun or mercy. I plucked one jet feather from my hood and left in his forehead, for, his, head.

For a souvenir, for a warning, for a lick of night in the morning.
For a little break in the mourning.

(Porter 2015: 10)

1 What is unusual about the noun profiles in the extract? In your answer, you might want to consider the following:

  a The inclusion/omission of definite/indefinite determiners;
  b Reference point relationships and nominal compounds;
  c The inclusion of count/mass nouns.

2 Drawing on some of the ideas from Chapter 2, how are the conceptual domains represented and re-appropriated? What metaphors can you identify in the passage?

3 What verb profiles can you identify? How do they contribute to, or detract from, the semantic cohesion?

Scanning poetry
Read Text 8F, three examples of Japanese Haiku:

Text 8F

In the twilight rain
these brilliant-hued hibiscus –
A lovely sunset.

— Basho Matsuo (1644–94)

A summer river being crossed
how pleasing
with sandals in my hands!

— Yosa Buson (1716–84)

A mountain village
under the piled-up snow
the sound of water.

— Masaoka Shiki (1867–1902)

1 What are these poems about? What conceptual domains do we draw on in order to understand them?

2 Do we read these poems via a summary or a sequence scan? What is the effect of this?

3 Rewrite one of the poems by adding more verb profiles, and compare your edit to the original. Does this change how we read the poem?

8.3.4 Chapter 5 Clauses

Default viewing arrangements and unnatural narration
The following are two examples of 'impossible' or 'unnatural' narrators in fiction about the Second World War: *The Book Thief* by Markus Zusak and *Slaughterhouse 5* by Kurt Vonnegut.

Chapter 5 defined fictive simulation as the idea that we can imagine events described in clauses, even if we do not have a direct frame of reference for them. In other words, we can construe events that we have not directly experienced.

Text 8G

DEATH AND CHOCOLATE

First the colours. Then the humans. That's usually how I see things. Or at least, how I try.

***HERE IS A SMALL FACT ***
You are going to die.

I am in all truthfulness attempting to be cheerful about this whole topic, though most people find themselves hindered in believing me, no matter my protestations. Please, trust me. I most definitely *can* be cheerful. I can be amiable. Agreeable. Affable. And that's only the As. Just don't ask me to be nice. Nice has nothing to do with me.

***REACTION TO THE AFOREMENTIONED FACT ***
Does this worry you?
I urge you – don't be afraid.
I'm nothing if not fair.

Of course, an introduction.
A beginning.
Where are my manners?
I could introduce myself properly, but it's not really necessary. You will know me well enough and soon enough, depending on a diverse range of variables. It suffices to say that at some point in time, I will be standing over you, as genially as possible. Your soul will be in my arms. A colour will be perched on my shoulder. I will carry you gently away.

At that moment, you will be lying there (I rarely find people standing up). You will be caked in your own body. There might be a discovery; a scream will dribble down the air. The only sound I'll hear after that will be my own breathing, and the sound of the smell, of my footsteps.

The question is, what colour will everything be at that moment when I come for you? What will the sky be saying?

Personally, I like a chocolate-coloured sky. Dark, dark chocolate. People say it suits me. I do, however, try to enjoy every colour I see – the whole spectrum. A billion or so flavours, none of them quite the same, and a sky to slowly suck on. It takes the edge off the stress. It helps me relax.

(Zusak 2005: 13–14)

Text 8H

The formation flew backwards over a German city that was in flames. The bombers opened their bomb bay doors, exerted a miraculous magnetism which shrunk the fires, gathered them into cylindrical steel containers, and lifted the containers into the bellies of the planes. The containers were stored neatly in racks. The Germans below had miraculous devices of their own, which were long steel tubes. They used them to suck more fragments from the crewmen and planes. But there were still a few wounded Americans, though, and some of the bombers were in bad repair. Over France, though, German fighters came up again, made everything and everybody as good as new.

(Vonnegut 1991: 53–4)

1   While fictive simulation occurs frequently when we read fiction, how do we recognize that these are impossible or unnatural narrators?

2   How has the default viewing arrangement been manipulated in each of these examples? How has this impacted on the construction of clauses/representation of grammatical roles, if at all?

3   Thinking back to other ideas introduced in this book, are there any other concepts of cognitive grammar that enable you to explore the representation of the character's voice, in particular? Given the subject matter, how do the alternative viewing arrangements represented in these extracts impact on our interpretation of the texts?

8.3.5 Chapter 6 Grounding

Read Text 8I, the poem 'Catching Fire' by Nigel McLoughlin.

Text 8I

She maintained only one right way
to clean the flue: fire shoved
up to burn it out, drive sparks
from the chimney stack and smuts
into air. Each bunched and bundled
paper held till the flame took
and it flew, took off on its own

consumption, rose on its own updraft.
I stood fixed by her leather face
dancing in firelight, her hands
clamped to the metal tongs.
Eyes stared black and wide, rims
of blue that circled wells, pools
that fire stared into. I watched
her pull from beneath them black
ash and a paper smell I love still.
She told me she saw faces in the flame
and people, places, things take place.
She'd spey fortunes there. Told me mine
but I saw nothing more or less
than the dance of flame, the leap
and die, the resurrection of yellow
cowl and dual change of split-
levelled flame that held within it
a dance of words, a ballet of images.
I heard only the music of burning
a soundless consummation of persistence
imagined a vision of my hands reddening
felt my knuckles braising
my bones in tongues, flaming.

(McLoughlin 2009)

1 What do you notice about the use of particular nominal and clausal grounding strategies in this poem? Identify and classify the ways in which grounding occurs based on your reading of Chapter 6.

2 What effect do they have in terms of presenting the experience of the speaker and how do they contribute to your interpretation of the poem?

Modality in weather forecasts

In Chapter 6, we examined how cognitive grammar treats modality in relation to a model of reality as a conceptualizer moves through time. Text 8J is an extract from a newspaper weather forecast that draws on various modal constructions.

Text 8J: Weather forecast

GENERAL SITUATION A warm airmass in southern Britain will result in the development of showers this morning, possibly heavy and thundery. A largely dry day will then follow for most places. However, low pressure to the south of Iceland will move eastwards over northern Scotland through the day, this will allow a cold front to gradually push south-eastwards across parts of western Scotland later in the day. **NW Scotland, N Isles, W Isles, NE Scotland, SW Scotland, SE Scotland:** A largely dry day, but a few showers are possible. It will be generally cloudy and it will feel fresher. However, later on in the

day, rain will spread in to western Scotland and this rain will become more widespread across Scotland this evening. Breezy with the heaviest rain in the west. Max temp: 19C. Tonight, rain will persist. Min temp: 9C.
Republic of Ireland, N Ireland: Drizzle should clear eastwards to leave a largely dry day. North-western and western areas will see cloud persisting, however areas further east will see some sunny intervals. Later in the day rain will move in from the west and this will continue into the evening. Light westerly winds. Max temp: 19C. Tonight, rain continues. Min temp: 12C.

Cen S England, SE Eng, Channel Is, London, East Anglia, Midlands: Showers gradually easing away eastwards to join much of the rest of the UK in drier but fresher weather. For much of the afternoon and evening, most places should remain dry with just a few possible showers along the eastern coast. Light north-westerly winds. Max temp: 28C. Tonight, largely dry. Min temp: 12C.
NW Eng, NE Eng, E Eng, IoM: Morning showers, these mainly in eastern areas, with some heavy and thundery showers possible too. Through the day, most showers should clear into the

North Sea and skies will become clearer to reveal some afternoon sunshine. A dry evening will follow. Generally light north-westerly winds. Max temp: 21C. Tonight, rain after midnight. Min temp: 11C.
N Wales, S Wales, SW England: Showers are expected during the morning, these could be heavy and thundery. Through the rest of the day it will become increasingly bright and it should become dry, but there will still be a fair amount of cloud in places. A partly cloudy and largely dry evening will then follow. Light winds. Max temp: 23C. Tonight, remaining dry. Min temp: 11C.

(*The Metro* 22 June 2017)

1 Identify the modal constructions that are used in this forecast and describe them in terms of how they express varying degrees of certainty, knowledge and understanding.

2 To what extent can you use cognitive grammar's 'model of reality' to account for the *style* of a weather forecast? You could also find additional examples of this type of text to support your claims.

8.3.6 Chapter 7 Discourse

Spoken discourse and CDS construction in *The Rosie Project*

Text 8K is an extract from Graeme Simsion's *The Rosie Project*. The protagonist, Don Tillman, is a professor in genetics who has been asked to present a guest lecture on Asperger's syndrome. He is covering for his friend, Gene, who is skiving. This scene describes him arriving in the lecture theatre and meeting the convenor, Julie.

Text 8K

'You must be Julie,' I said.

'Can I help you?'

Good. A practical person. 'Yes, direct me to the VGA cable. Please.'

'Oh,' she said. 'You must be Professor Tillman. I'm so glad you could make it.'

She extended her hand but I waved it away. 'The VGA cable, please. It's 6:58.'

'Relax', she said. 'We never start before 7.15. Would you like a coffee?'

Why do people value others' time so little? Now we would have the inevitable small talk. I could have spent fifteen minutes at home practising aikido.

I had been focusing on Julie and the screen at the front of the room. Now I looked around and realised that I had failed to observe nineteen people. They were children, predominantly male, sitting at desks. Presumably these were the victims of Asperger's syndrome. Almost all of the literature focuses on children.

Despite their affliction, they were making better use of their time than their parents, who were chattering aimlessly. Most were operating portable computing devices. I guessed their ages as between eight and thirteen. I hoped they had been paying attention in their science classes, as my material assumed a working knowledge of organic chemistry and the structure of DNA.

I realised that I had failed to reply to the coffee question.

'No.'

Unfortunately, because of the delay, Julie had forgotten the question. 'No coffee,' I explained. 'I never drink coffee before 3.48 pm. It interferes with sleep. Caffeine has a half-life of three to four hours, so it's irresponsible serving coffee at 7.00 pm. unless people are planning to stay awake until after midnight. Which doesn't allow adequate sleep if they have a conventional job.' I was trying to make use of the waiting time by offering practical advice, but it seemed that she preferred to discuss trivia.

'Is Gene alright?' she asked. It was obviously a variant on that most common of formulaic interactions 'How are you?'

'He's fine, thank you,' I said, adapting the conventional reply to the third-person form.

'Oh. I thought he was ill.'

'Gene is in excellent health except for being six kilograms overweight. We went for a run this morning. He has a date tonight, and he wouldn't be able to go out if he was ill.'

Julie seemed unimpressed.

(Simsion 2013: 7)

1 How is humour created in this extract?
2 How is the CDS structured in this scene? What factors are shared/not shared between the two discourse participants?
3 Does the CDS model work as successfully for prose fiction (as compared, for example, with a spoken transcript or dialogue from a play)?
4 In other words, are there any other ideas from cognitive grammar that might help you to analyse this scene in greater detail? You might want to consider, for example, the objectivity/subjectivity of the presented construal; the level of specificity in the language choices, and so forth.

Discourse structure in graphic novels

The following images (Text 8L) are taken from the graphic novel, *The Rime of the Modern Mariner*, which is a re-write of Coleridge's 'The Rime of the Ancient Mariner'.

Text 8L: Pages from *The Rime of the Modern Mariner*

(Hayes 2011)

1 The protagonist is in despair at this moment in the narrative. How is the protagonist's subjective construal shown through multimodal cues?

2 Do we process these pictorial frames as a summary or sequence scan, or both?

3 How do the images interact with the text?

8.4 Further discussion questions

1 Cognitive grammar has been hitherto received divisively. Criticisms can be traced to evaluations of the model as being overly complex, and therefore unwieldy or impractical as an analytical framework. Do you agree with these criticisms? How might you circumnavigate these difficulties in your own stylistic analysis?

2 The question of embodiment is interesting to analyse in respect of cultural variation. Can you find examples of how different cultures conceive of and construe concepts such as 'front' and 'back' and 'time'? What implications do you think that this has for stylistic analysis drawing on cognitive grammar?

3 To what extent do you think that context influences and affects construal? Find examples of literary texts that were written and/or have been read and interpreted in very specific contexts. Analyse the text or any response to it you have found using cognitive grammar. How well do you think that cognitive grammar as a framework for analysis can handle context?

4 The introduction of the reference point model in this chapter asked you to consider a couple of multimodal texts: an extract from a children's book and a political cartoon. Can you think of any multimodal contexts where reference point relationships are manipulated? Would you say this was a pervasive phenomenon in everyday discourse?

5 Chapter 5 observed that we construct clauses in order to represent our experience and understanding of the world around us. Original work in cognitive grammar explained how this works within the context of spoken discourse, or a particular exchange between a linguistic producer and a linguistic receiver. How does fiction manipulate the idea of the default viewing arrangement? You may want to think about the last book that you read as a way of framing your response.

6 Examine cognitive grammar's 'model of reality' in more detail by considering the extent to which you think it can account for the so-called unnatural narratives, that is narratives that project stories, events, characters, places and time sequences that cannot exist in the actual world. Can you think of any specific examples of literary texts that provide interesting examples when analysed using cognitive grammar's treatment of knowledge?

7 Stylistics is often described as a 'tool-kit' discipline. What does
cognitive grammar offer the stylistics tool-kit? If you are familiar
with other discourse frameworks in cognitive stylistics (such as
Text World Theory, contextual frame theory, etc.) in the field, you
might want to draw on these to help you answer. Do you think that
cognitive grammar can help support these existing stylistic models
(and vice versa)?

8.5 Selected key texts

8.5.1 Texts specifically about or using cognitive grammar

Browse, S. (2018), *Cognitive Rhetoric: The Cognitive Poetics of Political Discourse,* **Amsterdam: John Benjamins.**
This book explores political discourse through the lens of cognitive stylistics
and uses cognitive grammar as a key analytical method. Chapter 4 focuses
on construal, re-construal and resistant reading, while Chapter 7 examines
grounding.

Gavins, J. and G. Steen, eds (2003), *Cognitive Poetics in Practice,* **London: Routledge.**
This is the companion volume to the first edition of Stockwell's *Cognitive Poetics* and includes a range of cognitive stylistic analyses of different texts.
Chapter 5 contains Craig Hamilton's use of cognitive grammar to analyse
Wilfred Owen's poem 'Hospital Barge'.

Harrison, C., L. Nuttall, P. Stockwell and W. Yuan, eds (2014), *Cognitive Grammar in Literature,* **New York: Benjamins.**
This edited collection provides a range of examples of stylistic analyses using
cognitive grammar across different text types and genres. The introduction
offers a good overview of the value of cognitive grammar as a method of
analysis.

Harrison, C. (2017), *Cognitive Grammar in Contemporary Fiction,* **New York: Benjamins.**
This monograph takes cognitive grammar and applies it to provide detailed
chapter-length stylistic analyses of contemporary literature: the novels
Enduring Love by Ian McEwan, *The New York Trilogy* by Paul Auster and

Coraline by Neil Gaiman; a multimodal chapter from *A Visit from the Goon Squad* by Jennifer Egan; and the short story 'Here We Aren't, So Quickly' by Jonathan Safran Foer.

Langacker, R. (2008), *Cognitive Grammar: A Basic Introduction*, Oxford: Oxford University Press.
In this book, Langacker provides an introduction to cognitive grammar that draws on his many years of research and writing in the field. The book provides an introduction to the principles and parameters of Langacker's model together with worked examples and diagrams that outline principles. This book is challenging but provides a very good overview of the field and covers all of the topics addressed in this textbook in detail.

Nuttall, L. (2018), *Mind-style and Cognitive Grammar: Language and Worldview in Speculative Fiction*, London: Bloomsbury Academic.
Nuttall's monograph is a detailed study of the language of speculative fiction with a specific focus on cognitive grammar. Her discussion includes a comparison of cognitive grammar and systemic-functional grammar and an exploration of construal in relation to the representation of mind style.

Radden, G., and R. Dirven (2007), *Cognitive English Grammar*, Amsterdam: John Benjamins.
This is a more user-friendly book than Langacker's with plenty of examples and activities and detailed coverage of different aspects of grammar and cognition together with suggestions for further reading. It covers cognitive approaches to language more generally rather than being exclusively on Langacker's model of cognitive grammar.

Stockwell, P. (2019), *Cognitive Poetics*, 2nd edn, London: Routledge.
Now in its second edition, Stockwell's seminal work in cognitive poetics is a must-read for anyone interested in cognitive linguistic approaches to literary study. Each chapter provides a detailed overview of theory, a detailed analysis of a text and ideas for further work and reading. There is a chapter on cognitive grammar, updated from the first edition.

Stockwell, P. (2009), *Texture: A Cognitive Aesthetics of Reading*, Edinburgh: Edinburgh University Press.
This book takes familiar literary concepts such as characterization and tone and re-evaluates them from a cognitive stylistic perspective. There are references to and analyses of texts using ideas from cognitive grammar throughout. Chapter 6 contains specific analyses using cognitive grammar of 'Daffodils' by William Wordsworth and extracts from *Bleak House* by Charles Dickens and *Lord of the Rings* by J. R. R. Tolkien.

Taylor, J. (2002), *Cognitive Grammar,* **New York, NY: Routledge.**
Taylor's comprehensive book introduces cognitive grammar through discussion and analysis of a range of topics in different areas of language study. In a similar way to Radden and Dirven's volume, each of the chapters has questions and suggestions for further reading.

8.5.2 Texts on cognitive linguistics or demonstrating cognitive stylistic analysis more generally

Evans, V. and M. Green (2006), *Cognitive Linguistics: An Introduction,* **Edinburgh: Edinburgh University Press.**
The volume provides a thorough overview of the principles and parameters of cognitive linguistics, including sections on cognitive semantics and cognitive grammar.

Gavins, J. (2007), *Text World Theory: An Introduction,* **Edinburgh: Edinburgh University Press.**
Gavins' book is the best account of Text World Theory, a cognitive model of discourse processing. The book includes analyses of a number of literary and non-literary texts from a text-worlds' perspective.

Giovanelli, M. (2013), *Text World Theory and Keats' Poetry: The Cognitive Poetics of Desire, Dreams and Nightmares,* **London: Bloomsbury Academic.**
This is the first book-length treatment of a canonical English poet using Text World Theory. Chapters 4 and 5 integrate aspects of grounding from cognitive grammar into a discussion of modality and Keats' poem 'The Eve of St Agnes'.

Goldberg, A. (1995), *Construction: A Construction Grammar Approach to Argument Structure,* **Chicago: Chicago University Press.**
Goldberg's book provides an overview of her own construction grammar which, like Langacker's model, highlights how grammatical structures carry inherent meaning potential.

Littlemore, J., and J. R. Taylor, eds (2014), *The Bloomsbury Companion to Cognitive Linguistics,* **London: Bloomsbury.**
This edited collection contains chapters on various topics in cognitive linguistics and is a useful starting point for exploring different aspects of the field. This volume includes a chapter on cognitive poetics by Chloe Harrison and Peter Stockwell.

Simpson, P. (2014), *Stylistics: A Resource Book for Students,* **2nd edn, London: Routledge.**
This is a comprehensive overview of stylistics as a discipline and of the various tools and frameworks available to the stylistician. Simpson includes a number of sections on cognitive stylistics as well as some key readings from the field.

Ungerer, F., and H. J. Schmid (2006), *An Introduction to Cognitive Linguistics,* **2nd edn, Harlow: Longman.**
Ungerer and Schmid's book is a detailed yet very accessible introduction to cognitive linguistics and covers a number of its important topic areas. Activities and suggestions for further reading are provided to offer additional support.

Glossary

action chain in clauses, action chains describe how energy is transferred from one grammatical participant to another.

agent a participant in a clause that initiates an action or a process. An agent is seen as the energy source within a clause.

archetypal role a grammatical role that designates participants in terms of where they appear in the action chain (e.g. whether they are performing an action, receiving one, what type of process is being described, etc.).

category a group of concepts (and words to describe those concepts) that are defined in relation to each other and have relative degrees of membership.

circumstances additional information in a clause that describes the time or manner in which a process takes place.

clause generally speaking, clauses are units of language that are headed by a verb process.

clausal grounding the process by which an instance of an event or its reality status is made clear through the tensing of a verb or the addition of some kind of modality.

cognitive clause a clause that designates a verb of cognition or perception.

conceived reality the events that a conceptualizer knows about and establishes as having happened in the past.

conceived scene the event(s) that is construed by conceptualizers.

conceptual base the background content evoked by an expression which provides the context for understanding the profiled aspect.

conceptual metaphor a type of construal in which one concept is understood in terms of another.

conceptualizer the participants involved in construing an event, speaker/writer and hearer/reader.

construal the presentation of conceptual content. In cognitive grammar, a central idea is that there is the possibility for content to be construed in different ways, all of which are meaningful.

construction a structure in language which is made up of symbolic units of form and meaning.

coordinated mental reference the act of directing attention to the conceptual so that there is shared understanding, which allows effective communication to take place.

count noun typically physical objects, count nouns are things that can be counted and grouped. Count nouns therefore can take the plural form when more than one instance of the same type is listed.

covert grounding a grounding strategy where the grounding element singles out its referent indirectly, intrinsically or through the use of a zero-form.

current discourse space (CDS) a mental space that carries information about the wider context and shared knowledge of an interaction. We mentally build and adapt the CDS in order to interpret ongoing discourse events. It is made up of information that we have encountered previously in the interaction (known as the minus frames of the conversation), as well as information we anticipate about what will occur in the rest of the interaction to come (the plus frames of the conversation).

deictic verb a verb that denotes movement towards or away from a conceptualizer and therefore assumes a particular vantage point.

default viewing arrangement the idea that clauses are made prototypically by two speakers, in the same location, who are discussing or commenting on their surroundings or what is happening around them.

determiner determiners are paired with nouns in order to identify a particular instance in language. This can be done with greater or lesser specificity, using either a definite (e.g. 'the') or an indefinite (e.g. 'a') determiner respectively.

dictionary view of meaning the view that a definition of a word is simply that contained in a dictionary.

distal demonstrative a type of determiner that when used as a grounding element encodes a degree of distance between conceptualizer and referent.

ditransitive clause a clause that has three participants.

domain a wide, general area of knowledge against which individual words are used and understood.

domain matrix a set of several interrelated domains that may be evoked by a single word or expression.

dominion a reference point has many potential targets. These form the dominion of an expression.

dynamic clause clauses that describe something that happens. The simplest way of thinking about these clauses is to consider verbs of movement or action.

elaboration 1. a variation of a basic image schema; 2. an extension of a particular word in a chain where each part is relatively more specific than the one that precedes it.

elaborative relation a term to describe the various possible words, phrases or clauses that form a chain of terms as a result of elaboration.

embodiment how our use and understanding of language is shaped by our physical experience with the world

encyclopaedic view of meaning the view that posits that words act as access points to stores of knowledge that are based on our experience in the world. Meaning is therefore related to the way a word is used.

energy source the part of an action chain which initiates or performs the verb process, such as an agent.

energy sink the part of an action chain that receives the energy and is affected by it, such as a patient.

experiencer a participant in a clause, usually a person or a sentient entity, who experiences something. This role is categorized by verbs of perception or cognition, or by a mental or emotive process.

event time the time frame within which an event takes place.

evolutionary momentum the sense a conceptualizer has of moving through time and therefore perceiving reality in relation to the past, present and future.

fictive simulation a process that describes our ability to mentally simulate events that we have not directly experienced.

fictive vantage point an imagined (i.e. not directly experienced) viewing position from which events are construed.

figure/ground an overarching term for the relationship between an entity that is given prominence (figure) against a larger background (ground).

focus the particular part of the visual field that two interlocutors are paying attention to at any given moment in a conversation.

force dynamics a way of describing how entities act and interact in relation to different types of force.

frame a bundle of knowledge that we hold that is built up through direct or indirect experience.

gapping the act of excluding some aspects of a scene through a specific window of attention.

generality a term used to describe the effect of presenting aspects of a scene in non-specific ways.

goal the end point of a trajector moving along a path from a source.

gradience 1. the term used to describe the degrees of membership of a particular category, from a prototype to more peripheral members. 2. The term used to describe how different modal expressions denote varying degrees of obligation, permission, certainty, desire and ability.

granularity a term used to describe the effect of presenting aspects of a scene in specific ways.

ground the context or situation of a discourse event within which any form of communication takes place. This includes the participants (e.g. speaker and hearer), the immediate surrounding physical environment and the time of interaction.

grounding the process by which states and events in an utterance are fixed in relation to the current speech event, providing information about what happened, when it happened and who was involved.

grounding elements words or other forms (e.g. –ed morpheme) that function to bring about the process of nominal or clausal grounding.

image schema a schematic representation of activity that is built up from our everyday sensory experiences (vision, touch, movement, force and balance) and through which we understand our conceptual world.

immediate reality the events that a conceptualizer is aware of at the present moment in time.

immediate scope the part of a scene that is placed 'on stage' through a particular construal.

imperfective verb verbs that are not specifically bounded in time and are therefore used to identify a stable situation that continues through time.

indirect grounding a grounding strategy where the profiled instance is understood initially in relation to another entity, for example, in a possessive structure.

instance a noun that is a particular example from a wider category, and to which our attention is drawn through the inclusion of, for example, a definite determiner.

instantiation the process by which types become instances.

instrument a grammatical participant in a clause that is used by one participant to affect another. Usually, this is an inanimate object.

intransitive clause a clause that has one participant.

intrinsic grounding a grounding strategy that inherently profiles an instance of a type, for example through the use of a proper noun.

irreality the events that either have not happened or of which a conceptualizer has no knowledge whatsoever.

landmark the ground that acts as a reference point in a relational structure (phrase or clause).

linguistic rank scale the hierarchical structure of language, from small units (such as morphemes) to larger units (such as clauses).

locative the part of a clause that does not play an essential part in an action chain, but instead simply provides additional information about where the action occurs.

mapping the process by which correspondences come to exist between source and target domains.

mass noun nouns that cannot be counted or grouped, and therefore do not take the plural form when more than one instance is listed. Usually mass nouns are physical substances rather than objects.

maximal scope the wider domain evoked by a particular term and which provides the background for understanding it.

metonymy a process by which a concept is understood in terms of another concept within the same domain as opposed to a different domain (metaphor).

modality the ways in which we can create subjectivity in language. There are different modal senses such as deontic modality (obligation and permission); epistemic modality (certainty and possibility); boulomaic modality (desire); and dynamic modality (ability).

model of reality a schema by which we conceptualize events that have and have not happened, and judge the potential for events to happen (or not).

mover a participant in a clause that physically changes position or location.

nominal a group of words (phrase) that profiles a thing.

nominal grounding the process by which a particular instance of a thing is made accessible to the hearer of the utterance through specifying or quantifying a noun.

object of conception the conceptualized content in a particular construal.

objective construal a construal where more attention is afforded to the object of conception.

orientational metaphor a metaphor that is based on a spatial relationship between source and target domains.

overt grounding a grounding strategy where the grounding element singles out its referent explicitly.

participant roles grammatical roles held by parts of a clause.

path the direction taken by a trajector from a source to a goal.

patient a participant in a clause that undergoes a change of state.

perfective verb verbs that are bounded in time and that therefore single out a particular occurrence of an event.

potential reality the events that a conceptualizer believes could possibly happen.

primary focal participant the participant in a clause that receives the greatest attention, such as an agent.

principle of iconicity the premise that in cognitive grammar, there is a correspondence between a speaker's conceived reality and the grammatical forms used to express it.

profiling a term to describe the process of focusing attention on some aspect of a large structure.

projected reality the events that a conceptualizer is reasonably sure of occurring based on existing knowledge.

prototype the central member of a category.

proximal demonstrative a type of determiner that when used as a grounding element encodes a degree of closeness between conceptualizer and referent.

quantifier a word that indicates whether a noun is singular or plural. They can be proportional or can single out a representative instance of a noun.

reference point an identifiable or distinctive part of a scene. Reference points are useful for orientation in language, and allow us to identify and guide listeners' or readers' attention to less obvious parts of a scene.

referent the concept or thing referred to by a word.

set a number of elements that together form a larger mass.

scope the coverage a particular word or phrase gives to some aspect of its conceptual content.

secondary focal participant the participant in a clause that receives comparatively less attention, such as a patient.

sequence scanning the process by which we keep track of an event, at each successive stage, as it is happening. This occurs when we process perfective verbs.

source the starting point from which a trajector moves.

source domain the conceptual domain that is used to provide structure and expressions to the target domain.

specificity the degree to which we choose to zoom in or out on a particular scene.

speech time the time frame within which a conceptualizer speaks of an event taking place.

stative clause clauses that describe a situation in which no energy is created or exchanged between entities. Such clauses simply illustrate a state of affairs that exists or continues. Stative clauses can describe one entity in terms of another, can provide further identifying information about an entity or can outline the particular attributes of an entity.

subject of conception the conceptualizer of a particular construal.

subjective construal a construal where more attention is afforded to the subject of conception.

summary scanning the process by which we conceptualize a state within an event that occurs out of time with the real-time viewing experience. In a summary scan, we isolate one part of an event summatively. This occurs when we process imperfective verbs.

targets these are less distinctive or less salient parts of a scene. In order to guide a listener's attention to a target, we draw on more distinctive parts of the scene that are nearby.

target domain the conceptual domain that is afforded structure by and consequently understood through the source domain.

trajector the figure and most prominent element in a relational structure (phrase or clause) that is understood against the ground or landmark.

transitive clause a clause that has two participants.

type a noun phrase that represents a general category rather than a particular example within that category.

vantage point the viewing position a conceptualizer assumes in the act of construal.

viewing frame a viewing frame is the visual field of the speaker and hearer within a conversation.

voice the voice of a clause refers to whether it is active or passive.

windowing the focusing of attention on a particular aspect of a scene, leaving other aspects not available for viewing. In the case of a path of motion, windowing may be full (affording attention to the whole path), initial (affording attention to the starting point of the path), medial (affording attention to the middle section of the path) or final (affording attention to the end point of the path).

zero a participant in a clause that inhabits a static location.

zero-form a grounding strategy that omits any degree of specificity and instead diverts attention to the conceptual content of the referent itself.

References

Ahlberg, A. and A. Amstutz (2004), *Funnybones: The Pet Shop*, London: Puffin.

Auster, P. (1985), *City of Glass*, Los Angeles, CA: Sun & Moon Press.

Bennett, P. (2014), 'Langacker's Cognitive Grammar', in J. Littlemore and J. R. Taylor (eds), *The Bloomsbury Companion to Cognitive Linguistics*, 29–48, London: Bloomsbury.

Bergen, B. and N. Chang (2005), 'Embodied Construction Grammar in Simulation-based Language Understanding', in J. Östman and M. Fried (eds), *Construction Grammars: Cognitive Grounding and Theoretical Extensions*, 147–90, Amsterdam: John Benjamins.

Bonestell, J. (1995), 'A Second Chance', in S. Moss (ed.), *The World's Shortest Stories*, Philadelphia, PA: Running Press Book Publishers.

Broccias, C. and W. Hollman (2007), 'Do We Need Summary and Sequential Scanning in (Cognitive) Grammar?', *Cognitive Linguistics*, 18 (4): 487–522.

Browning, R. ([1849] 1989), 'Meeting at Night', in D. Karlin (ed.), *Selected Poems*, London: Penguin.

Browse, S. (2014), 'Resonant Metaphor in *Never Let Me Go*', in C. Harrison, L. Nuttall, P. Stockwell and W. Yuan (eds), *Cognitive Grammar in Literature*, 69–82, Amsterdam: John Benjamins.

Browse, S. (2016), 'Revisiting Text World Theory and Extended Metaphor: Embedding and Foregrounding Metaphor in the Text-worlds of the 2008 Financial Crash', *Language and Literature*, 25 (1): 8–37.

Browse, S. (2018), *Cognitive Rhetoric: The Cognitive Poetics of Political Discourse*, Amsterdam: John Benjamins.

Burke, M., ed. (2014), *The Routledge Handbook of Stylistics*, London: Routledge.

Carver, R. ([1983] 2003), 'Careful', in *Cathedral*, London: Vintage.

Chapman, S. and B. Clark, eds (2014), *Pragmatic Literary Stylistics*, London: Palgrave Macmillan.

Coates, J. (1983), *The Semantics of the Modal Auxiliaries*, London: Croom Helm.

Collins, S. (2008), *The Hunger Games*, London: Scholastic.

Connolly, J. (2004), 'The Inn at Shillingford', in *Nocturnes*, London: Hodder & Stoughton.

Conrad, J. ([1907] 2007), *The Secret Agent*, London: Penguin.

Cox, B. and J. Forshaw (2016), *Universal: A Guide to the Cosmos*, London: Penguin Random House.

Croft, W. (2001), *Radical Construction Grammar: Syntactic Theory in Typological Perspective*, Oxford: Oxford University Press.

Croft, W. and A. Cruse (2004), *Cognitive Linguistics*, Cambridge: Cambridge University Press.

Dahl, R. ([1953] 1979), 'Edward the Conqueror', in *Tales of the Unexpected*, Harmondsworth: Penguin.

Dashner, W. (2011), *The Maze Runner*, Somerset: Chicken House.

Donne, J. ([1633] 1994), 'The Canonization', in C. A. Patrides (ed.), *The Complete English Poems*, London: J. M. Dent.

Donoghue, E. (2010), *Room*, London: Picador.

Duffy, C. (1993), 'Valentine', in *Mean Time*, Manchester: Anvil Press.

Du Maurier, D. ([1938] 2012), *Rebecca*, London: Virago.

Enright, A. (2016), *The Green Road*, London: Vintage.

Epstein, R. (2001), 'The Definite Article, Accessibility, and the Construction of Discourse Referents', *Cognitive Linguistics*, 12 (4): 333–78.

Esmaeili, P. and F. Asadi Amjad (2016), 'Textual Properties and Attentional Windowing: A Cognitive Grammatical Account of Gustav Hasford's *The Short-Timers*', *Journal of Literary Semantics*, 45 (2): 161–74.

Evans, V. and M. Green (2006), *Cognitive Linguistics: An Introduction*, Edinburgh: Edinburgh University Press.

Fauconnier, G. and M. Turner (2002), *The Way We Think: Conceptual Blending and the Mind's Hidden Complexities*, New York, NY: Basic Books.

Fillmore, C. (1968), 'The Case for Case', in E. Bach and R. T. Harms (eds), *Universals in Linguistic Theory*, 1–88, New York: Holt.

Fillmore, C. (1985), 'Frames and the Semantics of Understanding', *Quaderni de Semantica*, 6 (2), 222–54.

Fish, S. (1980), *Is There a Text in the Class? The Authority of Interpretative Communities*, Cambridge, MA: Harvard University Press.

Fitzgerald, F. S. ([1922] 2002), *The Great Gatsby*, New York: Simon & Schuster.

Fludernik, M. (1994), *The Fictions of Language and the Languages of Fiction*, London: Routledge.

Flynn, G. (2012), *Gone Girl*, London: Orion.

Fowler, R. (1977), *Linguistics and the Novel*, London: Methuen.

Gaiman, N. (2002), *Coraline*, London: Bloomsbury.

Gaiman, N. (2013), *The Ocean at The End of The Lane*, London: Bloomsbury.

Gavins, J. (2005), '(Re)thinking Modality: A Text World Perspective', *Journal of Literary Semantics*, 34 (2): 79–93.

Gavins, J. (2007), *Text World Theory: An Introduction*, Edinburgh: Edinburgh University Press.

Gavins, J. and E. Lahey, eds (2016), *World Building: Discourse in the Mind*, London: Bloomsbury.

Gavins, J. and G. Steen, eds (2003), *Cognitive Poetics in Practice*, London: Routledge.

Gibbons, S. (1937) 'Roaring Tower', in *Roaring Tower and Other Stories*, London: Longmans, Green and Co.

Gibbs, R. W. and H. L. Colston (1995), 'The Cognitive Psychological Reality of Image Schemas and Their Transformations', *Cognitive Linguistics*, 6 (4): 347–78.

Giovanelli, M. (2013), *Text World Theory and Keats' Poetry: The Cognitive Poetics of Desire, Dreams and Nightmares*, London: Bloomsbury Academic.

Giovanelli, M. (2014a), 'Conceptual Proximity and the Experience of War in Siegfried Sassoon's "A Working Party"', in C. Harrison, L. Nuttall, P. Stockwell and W. Yuan (eds), *Cognitive Grammar in Literature*, 145–59, Amsterdam: John Benjamins.

Giovanelli, M. (2014b), *Teaching Grammar, Structure and Meaning*, London: Routledge.

Giovanelli, M. (2018a), '"Something Happened, Something Bad": Blackouts, Uncertainties and Event Construal in *The Girl on the Train*', *Language and Literature*, 27 (1): 38–51.

Giovanelli, M. (2018b), 'Construing the Child Reader: A Cognitive Stylistic Analysis of the Opening to Neil Gaiman's *The Graveyard Book*', *Children's Literature in Education*, 49 (2): 180–95.

Giovanelli, M. and J. Mason (2018), *The Language of Literature: An Introduction to Stylistics*, Cambridge: Cambridge University Press.

Goldberg, A. (1995), *Construction: A Construction Grammar Approach to Argument Structure*, Chicago: Chicago University Press.

Goldberg, M. (2003) 'Comprehension Test', in Z. Smith (ed.), *The Burned Children of America*, 59–68, London: Penguin.

Gregoriou, C. (2009) *English Literary Stylistics*, Houndmills: Palgrave Macmillan.

Haddon, M. (2003), *The Curious Incident of the Dog in the Night-Time*, London: Random House.

Halliday, M. A. K. (1971), 'Linguistic Function and Literary Style: An Inquiry into the Language of William Golding's *The Inheritors*', in S. Chatman (ed.), *Literary Style: A Symposium*, 330–65, Oxford: Oxford University Press.

Halliday, M. A. K. (1973), *Explorations in the Functions of Language*, London: Edward Arnold.

Halliday, M. A. K. (1985), *An Introduction to Functional Grammar*, London: Edward Arnold.

Halliday, M. A. K. and R. Hasan (1976), *Cohesion in English*, London: Longman.

Halliday, M. A. K. and C. Matthiessen ([1985] 2013), *Introduction to Functional Grammar*, 3rd edn, London: Edward Arnold.

Hamilton, C. (2003), 'A Cognitive Grammar of "Hospital Barge" by Wilfred Owen', in J. Gavins and G. Steen (eds), *Cognitive Poetics in Practice*, 55–65, London: Routledge.

Hampe, B. (2005), 'Image Schemas in Cognitive Linguistics: Introduction', in B. Hampe and J. E. Grady (eds), *From Perception to Meaning: Image Schemas in Cognitive Linguistics*, 1–12, Berlin: Mouton de Gruyter.

Harder, P. (1996), *Functional Semantics: A Theory of Meaning, Structure and Tense in English*, Trends in Linguistics Studies and Monographs 87, Berlin: Mouton de Gruyter.

Harrison, C. (2014), 'Attentional Windowing in David Foster Wallace's "The Soul Is Not a Smithy"', in C. Harrison, L. Nuttall, P. Stockwell and W. Yuan (eds), *Cognitive Grammar in Literature*, 53–67, Amsterdam: John Benjamins.

Harrison, C. (2017a), *Cognitive Grammar in Contemporary Fiction*, Amsterdam: John Benjamins.

Harrison, C. (2017b), 'Finding Elizabeth: Construing Memory in *Elizabeth Is Missing* by Emma Healey'. *Journal of Literary Semantics*, 46 (2): 131–51.

Harrison, C. and L. Nuttall (forthcoming), 'Cognitive Grammar and Reconstrual: Re-experiencing Margaret Atwood's "The Freeze-Dried Groom"', in B. Neurohr and E. Stewart-Shaw (eds), *Experiencing Fictional Worlds*, Amsterdam: John Benjamins.

Harrison, C., L. Nuttall, P. Stockwell and W. Yuan, eds (2014), *Cognitive Grammar in Literature*, Amsterdam: John Benjamins.

Hart, C. (2013), 'Event-construal in Press Reports of Violence in Two Recent Political Protests: A Cognitive Linguistic Approach to CDA', *Journal of Language and Politics*, 12 (3): 400–23.

Hart, C. (2014a), 'Constructing Contexts Through Grammar: Cognitive Models and Conceptualization in British Newspaper Reports of Political Protests', in J. Flowerdew (ed.), *Discourse and Contexts*, 159–84, London: Continuum.

Hart, C. (2014b), *Discourse, Grammar and Ideology: Functional and Cognitive Perspectives*, London: Bloomsbury.

Hart, C. (2015), 'Viewpoint in Linguistic Discourse: Space and Evaluation in News Reports of Political Protests', *Critical Discourse Studies*, 12 (3): 238–60.

Hart, C. (2016), 'The Visual Basis of Linguistic Meaning and its Implications for Critical Discourse Studies: Integrating Cognitive Linguistic and Multimodal Methods', *Discourse & Society*, 27 (3): 335–50.

Hawkins, P. (2015), *The Girl on the Train*, London: Doubleday.

Hayes, N. (2011), *The Rime of the Modern Mariner*, London: Random House.

Healey, E. (2014), *Elizabeth Is Missing*, New York: Harper Collins.

Hidalgo-Downing, L. and B. Kraljevic-Mujic (2011), 'Multimodal Metonymy and Metaphor as Complex Discourse Resources for Creativity in ICT Advertising Discourse', *Review of Cognitive Linguistics*, 9 (1): 153–78.

Hidalgo-Downing, L., B. Kraljevic-Mujic and B. Núñez Perucha (2013), 'Metaphorical Creativity and Recontextualisation in Multimodal Advertisements on E-Business across Time', *Metaphor in the Social World*, 3 (2): 119–219.

Hill, S. (1992), *The Mist in the Mirror*, London: Vintage.

Hodge, R. and G. Kress (1988), *Social Semiotics*, Cambridge: Polity Press.

Jeffries, L. and D. McIntyre (2010), *Stylistics*, Cambridge: Cambridge University Press.

Johnson, M. (1987), *The Body in the Mind: The Bodily Basis of Meaning, Imagination and Reason*, Chicago, IL: Chicago University Press.

Kay, P. and C. J. Fillmore (1999), 'Grammatical Constructions and Linguistic Generalisations: The What's Doing X to Y? Construction', *Language* 75: 1–33.

Keats, J. (1898), 'This Living Hand', in H. B. Forman (ed.), *The Poetical Works of John Keats*, Oxford: Oxford University Press.

Kennedy, C. (1982), 'Systemic Grammar and its Use in Literary Analysis', in R. Carter (ed.), *Language and Literature: An Introductory Reader in Stylistics*, 82–99, London: G. Allen and Unwin.

King, S. ([1977] 2011), *The Shining*, London: Hodder.

Koller, V. (2009), 'Brand Images: Multimodal Metaphors in Corporate Branding Messages', in C. Forceville and E. Urios-Aparisi (eds), *Multimodal Metaphor*, 45–71, Berlin: Mouton de Gruyter.

Kövecses, Z. (2005), *Metaphor in Culture: Universality and Variation*, Cambridge: Cambridge University Press.

Kövecses, Z. (2006), *Language, Mind, and Culture: A Practical Introduction*, New York, NY: Oxford University Press.

Kövecses, Z. (2010), *Metaphor: A Practical Introduction*, 2nd edn, New York, NY: Oxford University Press.

Kövecses, Z. (2015), *Where Metaphors Come From*, New York, NY: Oxford University Press.

Kress, G. and T. van Leeuwen (1996), *Reading Images: The Grammar of Visual Design*, London: Routledge.

Lakoff, G. (1987), *Women, Fire and Dangerous Things: What Categories Reveal about the Mind*, Chicago, IL: Chicago University Press.

Lakoff, G. and Johnson, M. (1980), *Metaphors We Live By*, Chicago, IL: Chicago University Press.

Lakoff, G. and Johnson, M. (1999), *Philosophy in the Flesh: The Embodied Mind and Its Challenge to Western Thought*, New York, NY: Basic Books.

Lakoff, G. and Turner, M. (1989), *More Than Cool Reason: A Field Guide to Poetic Metaphor*, Chicago, IL: University of Chicago Press.

Lane, R. (2014), *Her*, London: Orion.

Langacker, R. (1987), *Foundations of Cognitive Grammar, Volume 1, Theoretical Prerequisites*, Stanford: Stanford University Press.

Langacker, R. (1991), *Foundations of Cognitive Grammar, Volume 2, Descriptive Application*, Stanford: Stanford University Press.

Langacker, R. (2008), *Cognitive Grammar: A Basic Introduction*, Oxford: Oxford University Press.

Levinson, S. C. (1983), *Pragmatics*, Cambridge: Cambridge University Press.

Littlemore, J. and J. R. Taylor, eds (2014), *The Bloomsbury Companion to Cognitive Linguistics*, London: Bloomsbury.

Mandler, J. (2004), *The Foundations of Mind: Origins of Conceptual Thought*, Oxford: Oxford University Press.

Martin, G. R. R. (2000), *A Storm of Swords*, London: Harper Collins.

Mason, J. (2014), 'Narrative', in P. Stockwell and S. Whiteley (eds), *The Cambridge Handbook of Stylistics*, 179–95, Cambridge: Cambridge University Press.

McEwan, I. ([1997] 2004), *Enduring Love*, London: Vintage.

McEwan, I. (2017), *Nutshell*, London: Vintage.

McLoughlin, N. (2009), 'Catching Fire', in *Chora: New and Selected Poems*, Matlock: Templar Poetry.

Mieville, C. (2011), *Embassytown*, London: Pan Books.

Miller, N. (2013), *Breathless: An American Girl in Paris*, Berkeley, CA: Seal Press.

Neary, C. (2014), 'Profiling the Flight of "The Windhover"', in C. Harrison, L. Nuttall, P. Stockwell and W. Yuan (eds), *Cognitive Grammar in Literature*, 119–32, Amsterdam: Benjamins.

Nesbit, E. ([1893] 2016), 'In the Dark', in *Horror Stories*, London: Penguin.

Ness, P. (2011), *A Monster Calls*, London: Walker Books Ltd.

Nuttall, L. (2014), 'Constructing a Text World for *The Handmaid's Tale*', in C. Harrison, L. Nuttall, P. Stockwell and W. Yuan (eds), *Cognitive Grammar in Literature*, 83–99, Amsterdam: Benjamins.

Nuttall, L. (2015), 'Attributing Minds to Vampires in Richard Matheson's *I Am Legend*', *Language and Literature*, 24 (1): 24–39.

Nuttall, L. (2018), *Mind-style and Cognitive Grammar: Language and Worldview in Speculative Fiction*, London: Bloomsbury.

Nuyts, J. (2006), 'Modality: Overview and Linguistic Issues', in W. Frawley (ed.), *The Expression of Modality*, 1–25, Berlin: Walter de Gruyter.

Owen, W. ([1920] 1994), 'Anthem for Doomed Youth', in J. Stallworthy (ed.), *The War Poems of Wilfred Owen*, London: Chatto & Windus.

Päivärinta, A. (2014), 'Foregrounding the Foregrounded: The Literariness of Dylan Thomas's "After the funeral"', in C. Harrison, L. Nuttall, P. Stockwell and W. Yuan (eds), *Cognitive Grammar in Literature*, 133–44, Amsterdam: John Benjamins.

Palmer, F. (2001), *Mood and Modality*, 2nd edn, Cambridge: Cambridge University Press.

Plath, S. (1963), *Ariel*, London: Faber & Faber.

Pleyer, M. and C. W. Schneider (2014), 'Construal and Comics: The Multimodal Autobiography of Alison Bechdel's *Fun Home*', in C. Harrison, L. Nuttall, P. Stockwell and W. Yuan (eds), *Cognitive Grammar in Literature*, 35–54, Amsterdam: John Benjamins.

Porter, M. (2015), *Grief Is the Thing with Feathers*, London: Faber & Faber.

Pullinger, K. (1998), 'The Good Ferry', in D. Birkett and S. Wheeler (eds), *Amazonian: The Penguin Book of New Women's Travel Writing*, London: Penguin.

Pullman, P. (1995), *Northern Lights*, London: Scholastic.

Radden, G. and R. Dirven (2007), *Cognitive English Grammar*, Amsterdam: John Benjamins.

Riggs, R. (2011), *Miss Peregrine's Home for Peculiar Children*, Philadelphia, PA. Quirk Books.

Rosch, E. (1975), 'Cognitive Representations of Semantic Categories', *Journal of Experimental Psychology: General*, 104: 192–233.

Rosch, E. (1978), 'Principles of Categorization', in E. Rosch and B. B. Lloyd (eds), *Cognition and Categorization*, 27–48, Hillside, NJ: Lawrence Erlbaum.

Rowling, J. K. (2005), *Harry Potter and the Half-blood Prince*, London: Bloomsbury.

Semino, E. (2008), *Metaphor in Discourse*, Cambridge: Cambridge University Press.

Shakespeare, W. ([1597] 2002), *Richard II*, ed. C. R. Forker, London: Bloomsbury.

Shakespeare, W. ([1597] 2011), *Romeo and Juliet*, ed. René Weis, London: Bloomsbury.

Shakespeare, W. ([1598] 2002), *King Henry the Fourth Part One*, ed. David Scott Kastan, London: Bloomsbury.

Shelley, P. B. ([1819] 2002), 'Love's Philosophy', in B. Woodcock (ed.), *Selected Poems and Prose*. Ware, Hertfordshire: Wordsworth Editions.

Shibatani, M. (1985), 'Passives and Related Constructions: A Prototype Analysis', *Language*, 61: 821–48.

Simpson, P. (1993), *Language, Ideology and Point of View*, London: Routledge.

Simpson, P. (2014a), *Stylistics: A Resource Book for Students*, 2nd edn, London: Routledge.

Simpson, P. (2014b), 'Just What is Narrative *Urgency*?', *Language and Literature*, 23 (1): 3–22.

Simsion, G. (2013), *The Rosie Project*, London: Penguin.

Smith, D. ([1949] 2004), *I Capture the Castle*, London: Vintage.

Sotirova, V., ed. (2015), *The Bloomsbury Companion to Stylistics*, London: Bloomsbury.

Southey, R. ([1820] 1876), 'The Cataract of Lodore', in *The Poetical Works of Robert Southey*, Longmans, Green and Co.

Stockwell, P. (2009), *Texture: A Cognitive Aesthetics of Reading*, Edinburgh: Edinburgh University Press.

Stockwell, P. (2014), 'War, Worlds and Cognitive Grammar', in C. Harrison, L. Nuttall, P. Stockwell and W. Yuan (eds), *Cognitive Grammar in Literature*, 18–34, Amsterdam: Benjamins.

Stockwell, P. (2015) 'Poetics', in E. Dabrowska and D. Divjak (eds), *Handbook of Cognitive Linguistics*, 432–52. Berlin: de Gruyter Mouton.

Stockwell, P. (2019), *Cognitive Poetics: An Introduction*, 2nd edn, London: Routledge.

Stockwell, P. and S. Whiteley, eds (2014), *The Cambridge Handbook of Stylistics*, Cambridge: Cambridge University Press.

Stoker, B. ([1897] 2011), *Dracula*, Oxford: Oxford University Press.

Sweetser, E. (1990), *From Etymology to Pragmatics: Metaphorical and Cultural Aspects of Semantic Structure*, Cambridge: Cambridge University Press.

Tabakowska, E. (2014), 'Point of View in Translation: Lewis Carroll's *Alice* in Grammatical Wonderlands', in C. Harrison, L. Nuttall, P. Stockwell and W. Yuan (eds), *Cognitive Grammar in Literature*, 101–18, Amsterdam: John Benjamins.

Talmy, L. (1988), 'Force Dynamics in Language and Cognition', *Cognitive Science*, 12: 49–100.

Talmy, L. (2000a), *Towards a Cognitive Semantics*, Vol. 1: *Concept Structuring Systems*, Cambridge: Cambridge University Press.

Talmy, L. (2000b), *Towards a Cognitive Semantics*, Vol. II: *Typology and Process in Concept Structuring*, Cambridge MA: The MIT Press.

Taylor, J. (2002), *Cognitive Grammar*, New York, NY: Routledge.

Thomas, J. (1995), *Meaning in Interaction: An Introduction to Pragmatics*, London: Longman.

Turner, M. (1998), *The Literary Mind: The Origins of Thought and Language*, New York, NY: Oxford University Press.

Ungerer, F. and H. J. Schmid (2006), *An Introduction to Cognitive Linguistics*, 2nd edn, Harlow: Longman.

van Vliet, S. (2009), 'Reference Points and Dominions in Narrative: A Discourse Level Exploration of the Reference Point Model of Anaphora', in V. Evans and S. Pourcel (eds), *New Directions in Cognitive Linguistics*, 441–64, Amsterdam: John Benjamins.

Verhagen, A. (2007), 'Construal and Perspectivization', in D. Geeraerts and H. Cuyckens (eds), *The Oxford Handbook of Cognitive Linguistics*, 48–81, Oxford: Oxford University Press.

Verspoor, M. (1996), 'The Story of –ing: A Subjective Perspective', in M. Putz and R. Dirven (eds), *The Construal of Space in Language and Thought*, 417–54, Berlin: Walter de Gruyter.

Vonnegut, K. (1991), *Slaughterhouse Five*, New York: Dell Publishing.

Weldon, F. (1997), *Worst Fears*, London: Head of Zeus.

Werth, P. (1999), *Text Worlds: Representing Conceptual Space in Discourse*, London: Longman.

Wilde, O. ([1898] 1999), *The Importance of Being Earnest*, Cambridge: Cambridge University Press.

Wordsworth, W. ([1895] 1995), *The Prelude: The Four Texts*, London: Penguin.

Zusak, M. (2005), *The Book Thief*, London: Random House.

Index